Keys to the
Kingdom

*And New Dimensions
of Being*

Keys to the Kingdom
And New Dimensions of Being

Mark L. Prophet
Elizabeth Clare Prophet

SUMMIT UNIVERSITY PRESS®

KEYS TO THE KINGDOM AND NEW DIMENSIONS
OF BEING
Teachings of Mark L. Prophet and Elizabeth Clare Prophet
compiled by the editors of Summit University Press
Copyright © 2003 Summit University Press
All rights reserved

For information, please contact Summit University Press,
PO Box 5000, Corwin Springs, MT 59030-5000.
Tel: 1-800-245-5445 or 406-848-9500.
Web site: www.summituniversitypress.com
E-mail: info@summituniversitypress.com

Library of Congress Catalog Card Number: 2002113500
ISBN: 0-9720402-6-9

SUMMIT UNIVERSITY ✸ PRESS®

The Summit Lighthouse, Summit University Press, ✸, *Pearls
of Wisdom*, Teachings of the Ascended Masters, and Science of
the Spoken Word are registered trademarks.

Image of Elizabeth Clare Prophet on page 14 copyright ©
1999 Larry Stanley

Cover and interior design and production: Brad Davis

Printed in the United States of America
06   05   04   03   6   5   4   3   2   1

*Little keys unlock
the biggest doors,
and man
must be ready
to walk through
and not stand hesitatingly
upon the threshold.*
—EL MORYA

CONTENTS

Because gender-neutral language can be cumbersome and at times confusing, we have sometimes used *he* and *him* to refer to God or the individual. These terms are for readability only and are not intended to exclude women or the feminine aspect of the Godhead. Likewise, our use of *God* or *Spirit* does not exclude other expressions for the Divine.

KEYS TO THE KINGDOM

*T*his little book seeks to summarize forty years of teachings delivered through Mark and Elizabeth Clare Prophet. It provides an answer to the often-asked question, "Tell me in a nutshell: What is it that Mark and Elizabeth Prophet teach? What is the essence of their message?"

It is difficult to encapsulate the lifelong mission of these two remarkable people into one small book. Yet, the vastness of the message can be distilled into the Great Commandment— love for God, love for one's neighbor as oneself, love for the Christ and the Buddha within. It is the path walked by the saints of East and West for centuries.

The message is timeless, yet Mark and Elizabeth Clare Prophet give a new perspective on this message for a new millennium. In it you will find the keys that can unlock the door to your Inner Self. In it you will find the keys to your destiny on earth. In it you will find the spiritual keys for your journey Home to God.

Your soul has been waiting for this message for a long time. And yet, you did not need to look very far. The message was always there, close at hand—right inside you. It is the message of the Higher Self, the inner guide and the teacher within. It is the message of the heart.

Perhaps that is why many recognize this message when they hear it, finding it strangely familiar. "Why yes," they say, "I already know that. I have always known this eternal truth."

Behold, the days come, saith the LORD, that I will make a new covenant with the house of Israel and with the house of Judah.... I will put my law in their inward parts, and write it in their hearts; and will be their God, and they shall be my people.[1]

THE MESSENGERS

For every message from the realms of light, there is a messenger. The task of the messenger is to bring the message of truth from those realms to embodied mankind. Mark and Elizabeth Prophet are two such messengers, and their mission is to bring a new gospel for this age. It is the Everlasting Gospel foreseen by the author of Revelation.

To be a messenger is a special calling from God. Messengers do not come along every day, nor is their task an easy one. It is hard to bring a message of Truth to mankind. Most of us would rather not hear that we should change or move from our comfort zone. But God has always sent his messengers as wayshowers, to light the way on the spiritual path, exhorting mankind to return to him.

Mark and Elizabeth Clare Prophet

Ultimately, the concept of a messenger is a simple one. A messenger is a reminder, sent to remind you of what you already know and who you really are: you are a great and powerful spiritual being; you have come from heaven, and to heaven you are destined to return.

A UNIQUE ROLE

*E*lizabeth Clare Prophet has described her role as messenger in the following way:

"My calling is to be a prophet of God. Prophet means one who speaks for God, hence, a messenger. Coincidentally (although I don't believe in coincidences), my name matches my calling. Prophet is the surname of my late husband and teacher, Mark L. Prophet. It was the family name that had been carried through generations from France to Ireland to Canada to Chippewa Falls, Wisconsin.

"Mark was a prophet and a messenger, called by God through the ascended master El Morya to found The Summit Lighthouse in Washington, D.C., in 1958. He was and is the most amazing person I've ever met—the most humble, the most holy, the most human.

"We were together for 12 years, were married, had four children, wrote many books, lectured around the world and built our movement. And then he passed on in 1973, his soul now one with God, yet ever with me.

"In 1964, I received the 'mantle' of messenger, including gifts of the Holy Spirit. And throughout my ministry, by God's grace, I have built upon the foundation of prophetic teachings already laid by my husband.

"As a messenger of God, I see myself as the servant of God's light within you. And the servant is not greater than his lord. My Lord is the Christ of Jesus and the Christ of you, who are one and the same. For, as John the Beloved wrote, that Christ was and is 'the true Light, which lighteth every man that cometh into the world.'[2] Therefore, I come as a servant of that light—your light, my light, your Christ, my Christ."

CHAPTER 1
BEINGS OF LIGHT IN THE
REALMS OF HEAVEN

*M*any people who have been through a near-death experience speak of meeting wondrous beings of light while on the other side. Although some, such as Jesus, were easily identified, others did not reveal their name but simply flowed with love, compassion, teaching and guidance. Who are these masterful beings?

Let us take a look inside the heaven-world to gain some insight.

The Ascended Masters

Many of those you might meet in the heaven-world are known as ascended masters. The ascended masters are our elder brothers and sisters on the spiritual path. They have graduated from earth's schoolroom and returned to God. From the heaven-realm, they guide and teach mankind.

Many of these masters are familiar to us, having walked among us through the ages—others may be unknown to our outer mind. Since the dawn of time, these masterful beings have emerged from all races and nationalities, from all walks of life and all religions. Some of them are ancient beings of light, and their names have long ago became secondary to the flames they bear.

Whatever their origin in the vastness of our Father's universe, they all have something in common. They have balanced their misuse of God's energy (karma), accomplished their unique mission on earth and ascended back to the heart of God. One and all, they share a common light. These beloved ones form a part of the brotherhood of spiritual beings and angelic hosts known in heaven and on earth as the Great White Brotherhood.* They are spoken of in Revelation 7 as the great multitude of saints "clothed with white robes" who stand before

---

* White refers not to race or nationality but to the white light that surrounds the immortals. The Great White Brotherhood is a spiritual order of saints and adepts of every race, culture and religion. These masters have transcended the cycles of karma and rebirth and reunited with the Spirit of the living God.

the throne of God.

Among these saints are such well-known adepts as Gautama Buddha, Maitreya, Jesus Christ, Saint Michael the Archangel, Zarathustra, Moses, Melchizedek, Mother Mary, Teresa of Avila, Saint Francis, Saint Germain, Padre Pio and El Morya, to name just a few. Among their ranks are also unnumbered and unnamed loving hearts, servants of humanity who have returned Home and are a part of the living God forevermore.

The ascended masters are very much concerned with the evolutions of earth and the progress of the light in every area of human endeavor. Often working behind the scenes in the spiritual realm, the masters serve side by side with earnest seekers and public servants of every race, religion and walk of life to assist humanity in their forward evolution.

The ascended masters are teachers of mankind. They take a loving personal interest in their students and often intercede in their lives in many ways, both seen and unseen. They teach the path of overcoming victory where the soul can walk the earth with self-mastery, follow in the footsteps of Jesus or Buddha or other great lights, and return to the heaven-world at the conclusion of a lifetime of service. This is the path of personal Christhood whereby each one can find the way of overcoming.

This path is well marked by the footsteps of those who have gone before, and there are guides who can assist you in the steps that you need to take. They can point out the pitfalls and point out the easier way through the rough terrain. They have ropes and tools to assist you in the upward climb, and in the difficult places they offer a helping hand up and over the precipice. The guides cannot make the climb to the top of the mountain for you, but they are there to assist you in any way they can.

Having once walked where we now walk, the masters are well qualified to teach us. And even as they teach mankind, they are students of other masters who are above them in the great chain of being, the heavenly hierarchy. The path of discipleship continues in the heaven-world and is a model for the student-teacher, master-disciple relationship on earth.

Homes of Light
in the Heaven-World

The heaven-world is a vast and yet well-organized place. Among the sights you would see there are beautiful retreats and places of learning. An ascended master retreat is a focus of the Great White Brotherhood anchored in the etheric plane where the masters reside. (The etheric plane is simply a dimension that is above our physical, mental and emotional world. This dimension is of a higher vibration that we call heaven, or the ascended master octave.)

Just as we have earthly houses and cities, so there are homes and cities of light in the heaven-world. The retreat of a master might have many rooms or buildings, accommodating many souls and serving innumerable functions. There are rooms for council meetings where the masters gather to discuss the affairs of earth and heaven, temples for devotion and worship, centers for learning and repositories of the great wisdom of the ages, places of training for souls of light as they travel in their finer bodies during sleep or between embodiments, and places for rest at the conclusion of an earthly sojourn. As well as all of this, these retreats are anchoring points for certain spiritual energies on behalf of mankind.

Souls of mankind who are in embodiment and who desire to be trained are able to visit these retreats in their soul consciousness while their body sleeps. They come to learn and to study, to understand the circumstances of their lives and to prepare for the challenges of daily life in the schoolroom of earth. Many are consciously working at these inner levels to prepare for their life's calling or mission—their divine plan.

You may visit these retreats for some time before having a waking memory of your experience there. And although you may have just heard of the concept of an ascended master retreat, the retreats themselves are not new— they are ancient. The retreats and spiritual focuses of the Great White Brotherhood were established almost concurrently with the birth of the planet.

The retreats of the masters play an important role in the spiritual evolution of mankind. A retreat is more than a place where an ascended master lives and receives his students, or chelas. A retreat is a mandala, or a forcefield, that is used by the solar hierarchies to release increments of energy to a planet and a people. This light is necessary to the forward progression of life on the planet. The masters step down this light through their chelas for distribution among mankind. It is this light and energy that literally sustains the planet as a platform for the evolution of all those who live here.

There are very few sincere seekers for truth who have not already journeyed to these retreats. You may well have visited the retreats while your body slept at night, even though you

The Teton Range, Wyoming

had no outer memory of this experience.

One of the most frequently visited retreats is the Royal Teton Retreat. This retreat is located within the Teton mountain range near Jackson Hole, Wyoming. This vast and active center is the principal retreat of the Great White Brotherhood on the North American continent. It is an ancient focus of great light, in operation long before the sinking of Atlantis more than 12,000 years ago. It is a gathering place for the ascended masters and their disciples, even as many of the masters also maintain the specialized functions of their own retreats at other locations.*

The Royal Teton Retreat is the location of one of the Universities of the Spirit where thousands of unascended mankind attend classes of instruction each night. In these Universities they learn about cosmic law, the circumstances of their karma, their divine plan, the conditions on earth and other information vital to the ongoing evolution of the planet. When they awake from sleep, they are often inspired to urgently search on earth for what they remember from

---

* For more information about the Royal Teton Retreat and other retreats of the ascended masters, see *The Masters and Their Retreats*, by Mark and Elizabeth Clare Prophet.

the heavenly realm.

A simple request or prayer can enable the angels to take you to the masters' retreats while your body sleeps at night. Here is a prayer you can give to ask to be taken to the Royal Teton Retreat:

Prayer for Soul Travel

Father, into thy hands I commend my spirit.
Mighty I AM Presence and Holy Christ
Self, I call to Archangel Michael and his
legions of blue-lightning angels to protect and
transport my soul clothed in my finer bodies to
the Royal Teton Retreat near Jackson Hole,
Wyoming this night. Escort me, instruct me,
guide and protect me as I work to set free all
life on earth. I ask this be done in accordance
with the holy will of God.

The Seven Rainbow Rays

The path back to the Source can be walked over seven rays of the Christ consciousness that emerge from the white light.

Imagine a ray of white light entering a prism and dividing into seven rainbow rays. These are the natural division of the pure white light emanating from the heart of God as it descends through the prism of manifestation. These are the subdivisions of the wholeness of Christ.

The seven rays are outlined as follows:

(1) Blue—power and faith
(2) Yellow—wisdom and illumination
(3) Pink—love and beauty
(4) White—ascendancy and purity
(5) Green—science, healing and supply
(6) Purple and gold—ministration and service
(7) Violet—transmutation and diplomacy

The colors of the rays as they emerge from the white light remind us of Joseph's coat of many colors. Just as the seamless garment of the Lord Christ Jesus was white, so in his embodiment as Joseph, he wore the coat of many colors. The many became the one in the Christ, and out of that Christ light can be drawn forth the many colors of universal perfection. Regardless of their color, all of the rays have a white-fire core of purity that embodies all of the attributes of God.

Each day of the week there is released to the earth a special concentration of one of the seven rainbow rays of God. As these rays enter the physical world, they become a flame, bursting with energy to ignite a world in the seven colors of the rainbow.

We who would follow in the footsteps of Christ may meditate upon the colors of the rainbow rays of light's perfection.

Meditation on the Rainbow Rays

Blue is the flame of faith, promise, constancy, power, strength and of the earnestness and will of God. It flows out of vast luminous reservoirs into sea and sky. It is Tuesday's blessing to the earth.

Yellow is the merging of the gold and the white, imparting illumination, the consecration of right knowledge, the service of right knowledge, the outshining of the Christ mind and the establishment of the law of harmonious relations between all peoples and between God and all peoples. It is the ray of the sun sent to the earth on Sunday, the day of the sun.

Pink is the symbol of divine love. Love is joyous, buoyant and beautiful. Through the power of love, men learn how they may impart to others the beauty and the compassion they have received from God. Love is the require-ment of the hour. In the giving of this charity and beauty, there is no robbery, but only the fair exchange among all souls who are ennobled by the same love that God is. Monday is the day of the week that is imbued with the creative power of love.

The white ray of purity is composed of all of the colors of the rainbow. It has its own gigantic sheath that, as a sea of liquid flame, holds before the children of men the longing to be a part of that which can never be contaminated by reason or by deceitful act. The white light is the mind of God, the nature and character of God. It is freedom from stain and blame, the triumphant merging of the many colors into the purity of the One. Friday is the day when through purity man obtains his freedom from the bonds of limitation.

The ray of green imbues all life with the perfect blend of the yellow and the blue—the faith and wisdom of God in nature. The eternal newness of the color green charges man with the healthful and health-giving chlorophyl of the sun—the fire of the sun and the fire of the power to create. The healing green restores man to the primal nature of God. The ray of green supplies man with every lack and is the color of abundance and supply. It penetrates the earth on Wednesday, the day of healing and wholeness.

The purple and the gold imbue man with the desire for cosmic service. The colors are symbolic of the priesthood of true believers. The purple speaks of the illumined fire of the soul. This fire must assist every part of life to find reunion with its Source and with the golden law that God has dispensed to men. It is the ministration of the Christ to his disciples, of the servant who is not greater than his Lord. This twofold action of God's body (purple) and his essence (gold) bathes the earth on Thursday.

Finally, the violet ray synthesizes into action the rays of love and power, the pink and the blue, forming the radiance of the violet flame. Also called the royal purple, it shows the sense of the mantle aborning within the consciousness of man.

God has caressed and blessed the individual. Now that one must wear the mantle of the seventh ray, the robe of tact, diplomacy and of judgment. He must mediate as best he can for his fellow men, for those who have not yet advanced to his level of attainment. He must serve the cause of freedom and help deliver men from the bondages they themselves have created. He does not expect thanks, but holds in his grateful heart the feeling of gratitude for more service in order that tomorrow he may give in greater measure that which he has given in lesser measure today. The violet ray is amplified on Saturday—a day to pause and consider the meaning and ritual of freedom.

Discipleship Under
Seven Masters of Wisdom

The seven rainbow rays present seven paths to individual self-mastery, defined as the seven archetypes of Christhood. There are seven masters who have mastered identity by walking the paths of the seven rays and now stand to help others walk these paths.

These seven masters are known as the chohans of the seven rays. *Chohan* is a Sanskrit term for lord. The chohans define the law on their ray; through them that energy of the Christ and of God flows to mankind, to all who are evolving on that particular path.

The chohans are the closest ascended masters to us. They function in planes of perfection, but these planes are simultaneously one with the Matter plane where we are—there is a congruency of Spirit and Matter, and time and space are but coordinates of infinity. Therefore, you could say that the chohans are here with us.

All of the chohans are teachers of mankind. Each of them opens to you a path of discipline that corresponds to the ray and chakra (spiritual center) that that one represents. Let us look briefly at these seven chohans and their retreats.

El Morya, chohan of the first ray, maintains his focus of the will of God on the etheric plane concurrent with Darjeeling, India. He is the Chief of the Darjeeling Council, a council of ascended masters of the Great White Brotherhood.

Lanto is the lord of the second ray, the yellow ray of illumination. He serves in the Royal Teton Retreat. He is especially concerned with the education of the youth of the world.

Paul the Venetian is chohan of the third ray of divine love, the pink flame. He is the hierarch at the Château de Liberté in southern France. He sponsors the ascended master culture for this age and works with all who desire to bring that culture forth on behalf of mankind.

Next we come to the great disciplinarian, Serapis Bey, chohan of the fourth ray. Serapis maintains the focus of the Ascension Temple at Luxor in Egypt. This is the place where candidates for the ascension are received, and it is considered the most difficult retreat to enter. Serapis Bey is the teacher of the path to the ascension.

Hilarion is the chohan of the fifth ray, the green ray of precipitation and truth. He was embodied as the apostle Paul. He maintains the Temple of Truth on the etheric plane over the island of Crete, in Greece. He works especially with atheists, agnostics, skeptics and others who have become disillusioned with life and with religion.

The sixth ray of ministration and peace is presided over by Nada as chohan. The flame of the sixth ray is purple, the color of violets, flecked with metallic gold. Nada's retreat is in Saudi Arabia.

Saint Germain, chohan of the seventh ray, holds a very important position in hierarchy in this age. Not only is he the chohan of the seventh ray of freedom, mercy, transmutation and ritual, but he is also the hierarch of the Aquarian age. The pulsations of the violet flame can be felt from his etheric retreat over the Carpathian foothills in Romania and from the Cave of Symbols in the United States.

The offices of the seven chohans of the rays are divinely appointed by the cosmic hierarchy. Those who hold these offices are selected from among the most qualified ascended beings who have risen from earth's schoolroom. Each one has attained self-mastery and won the ascension by serving humanity on one or more of the seven rays through their embodiments in the world of form.

The chohan for each ray is responsible for the administration to mankind of all the aspects of their ray, while harmonizing their administration with the other six rays of the white light. The chohans always obey cosmic law; yet they are given certain latitude in keeping with their own individual evolution, capacities and endowments to direct mankind in the most adroit manner, giving loving assistance and spiritual direction as needed. Legions of angelic hosts and ascended brethren serve with them to carry out the plan of the Great White

Brotherhood for the most complete expression of the seven rays that is possible.

Mankind are keyed to certain rays in order that they may perform a specific service to God and man. Each of us "majors" on a particular ray, and we also have a "minor" ray on which we serve. Our ray may vary from one embodiment to the next, but the reward for service is cumulative, and thus powerful momentums may be retained from our past service on several or all of the rays. A balance of attainment on all of the seven rays is a requirement for the ascension and the mark of the golden-age man.

The services of the seven chohans impact all who work in the world whatever their level of service: statesmen, leaders and organizers are on the first ray under El Morya; teachers, philosophers and educators serve on the second ray under Lanto; artists, designers, beauticians and those of a creative nature serve on the third ray under Paul the Venetian; architects, planners and those dedicated to the purity and discipline of any undertaking serve with Serapis Bey on the fourth ray; doctors, scientists, healers, musicians, mathematicians and those consecrated to truth serve on the fifth ray with Hilarion; ministers, nurses and all who administer to mankind's needs assist Nada on the sixth ray; diplomats, priests of the sacred fire, actors, writers and defenders of freedom serve with Saint Germain on the seventh ray.

If we lack one of these godly attributes and want to make progress on a particular path back to God, we can pray to our God Presence, our own Holy Christ Self and the chohan of that ray for those qualities we want to see manifest in us. For example, we can pray to Paul the Venetian to assist us to develop more love in our life and to understand the true meaning of divine love so that we can better serve mankind.

By working with a chohan, we can make great strides of spiritual progress in a comparatively short time. If we are not certain what is our ray, it is best to begin with the first ray and the master El Morya. Morya prepares the students for their work with the other masters.

CHAPTER 2
THE REAL YOU

*Y*ou have a unique spiritual destiny. One of the keys to fulfilling that destiny is recognizing that you have a divine nature and a direct relationship with God.

You have a Higher Self, and you don't have to die and go to heaven to see your Higher Self! It is diagrammed in the Chart of Your Divine Self, which is a portrait of you and the God within you.

Dannion Brinkley, well-known author and expert on the near-death experience, could not believe his eyes when he saw this Chart while seated next to someone on a plane. He had previously seen his Real Self in his own near-death experience. He knew that whoever drew that Chart had been where he had been or had seen what he had seen.[3]

The Chart of Your Divine Self

The Chart is simple and yet profound. If we were able to take a photograph of you from a spiritual perspective, this is what you would look like. Your spiritual reality contains three figures, each corresponding to one of the three persons of the Trinity. The upper figure is your God Self. The middle figure is your Inner Teacher, or your Christ Self. And the lower figure is you as a soul evolving on earth.

Your I AM Presence

The upper figure in the Chart is your I AM Presence. It corresponds to the Father aspect of God. To Hindus it is Brahma. Buddhists call it the Dharmakaya, while Christians think of it as God the Father. It is the spirit of God individualized for each of us.

I AM THAT I AM is the name of God that he revealed to Moses on Mount Sinai. God told Moses, "I AM THAT I AM. Thus shalt thou say unto the children of Israel, I AM hath sent me unto you…. This is my name for ever, and this is my memorial unto all generations."[4] It is an ancient name, and yet we use it every day. Whenever we say the words, "I am," we are really saying "God in me."

According to your level of devotion, your I AM Presence may be very near or very far from you. When you draw near to God through loving thoughts, feelings and actions, your I AM Presence will draw near to you, just as the Epistle of James says, "Draw nigh to God and he will draw nigh to you."

Your I AM Presence is surrounded by seven concentric spheres of spiritual energy that make up what is called your "causal body." The spheres of pulsating energy contain the record of all the good works you ever have performed. They are like your cosmic bank account in heaven. The spheres in order from the center are white, yellow, pink, violet, purple and gold, green, and blue.

Your Holy Christ Self

The middle figure is your Inner Teacher, the Inner Christ. Your Christ Self can assist you every day in small ways and great. You can think of your Christ Self as your dearest friend and chief guardian angel. Just as the upper figure, the I AM Presence, is the Universal Presence of God the Father individualized for each one, so the Christ Self is the Universal Christ Presence within each one of us.

Sometimes people stumble or get hung up on the word *Christ*. This word comes from the Greek *Christos*, meaning "anointed." Hence, the Christed one is one who is anointed with the light of the Lord, the I AM Presence. If the word concerns you, you may substitute Buddha or Allah or Jehovah—whatever particular name you identify with.

The Christ Self is the voice that speaks within our heart—the still small voice of the hidden man of the heart. It is the voice of conscience that tells us right from wrong, giving unerring guidance and direction when we learn to listen.

The Christ Self is the Mediator between God and man, and corresponds to the second person of the Trinity, the Son of God. The Bible refers to Jesus Christ as the "Son of God" because Jesus became one with his Christ Self. In fact, the Father and the Son dwelt fully in Jesus, as he said and as Paul testified. The Christ Self is the Christ of Jesus and the Christ of you and me.

There is no record in the scriptures of Jesus saying that he is the only Son of God, having exclusive right to Divine Sonship. Where orthodoxy misses the boat is in its claim of an exclusive Divinity and an exclusive Sonship for Jesus that denies the God-potential and the Christ-potential to all other souls. It fails to see what John the Beloved saw, that every man (every *man*ifestation of God) that cometh into the world is ignited by the light of the same God and the same Christ who took up their abode in the temple of Jesus. "That was the true Light, which lighteth every man that cometh into the world."[5]

The difference between Jesus and the rest of us is that Jesus had the full attainment of that Godhead and that only begotten Son dwelling in him bodily. Since we have not yet perfected our Christhood in our souls or in our bodies of flesh, the I AM Presence and the Christ Self dwell above us (not in us) and go before us to light our way.

Every soul has a mission. Jesus' mission was to demonstrate the path of the soul's union with the I AM Presence and the Christ Self. He was the example of that which each of us must one day become. He is our Lord and Saviour because we have strayed far and wide from the house of the Father and the Son, and therefore, without his mediatorship, we of ourselves cannot enter into our true relationship with the Father and the Son, as illustrated on the Chart. Nor can we receive our divine inheritance without his grace.

Your Christ Self overshadows you wherever you are and wherever you go. That Christ Self endows you with the capacity to be "Christ conscious" at all times or, to put it another way, to have the "Christ consciousness" always.

The early Christian Gnostics, whose writings were suppressed by orthodoxy, taught the same principles. The Gospel of Philip describes the follower of Jesus who walks fully in his footsteps as "no longer a Christian but a Christ."[6] In the Gospel of Thomas, Jesus says, "He who will drink from my mouth will become like me. I myself shall become he."[7] You can think of Jesus as saying, "The 'I' that is the Christ in me is the same 'I' that is the Christ in you. Thus, when you shall have become (one with) the same Christ that I AM (for there is but one Christ) then I shall become you and you shall become me—*as I AM*."

Buddhist texts also speak of a divine nature that each soul can externalize. They describe it as "the Buddha essence" that is "in all beings at all times."[8] In the West, this concept of the potential incarnation of the light of God, of the Inner Buddha and the Inner Christ, in every child of God is not well known but is a part of the emerging spirituality of our time.

The Crystal Cord

The shaft of white light descending from the I AM Presence through the Christ Self to the lower figure is the crystal cord. John saw the crystal cord and described it as "a pure river of water of life, clear as crystal."[9] You can think of it as the "umbilical cord," the lifeline that ties you to your Higher Self. Through this cord, the light, energy and consciousness of God flow through you constantly, giving you life, breath and vitality. The light enters the body at the top of the head and nourishes and sustains the spiritual flame in the heart as well as the physical heartbeat and all bodily functions.

Your Four Lower Bodies

The lower figure in the Chart of Your Divine Self represents you, the aspirant on the spiritual path, enveloped in the violet flame, the spiritual fire of the Holy Spirit.

Each one of us has a soul, and the soul has an awareness that is integrated into every part of our body and even our finer bodies. We are not just our physical body. We are magnificent spiritual beings who happen to be wearing a physical body. But we also have other vehicles, other clothing for the soul. We think, we have feelings and desires, and we have a soul memory of the past that we bring with us. Thus, we have a mental body, a desire body and a memory body as well as a physical body. These four bodies are the "coats of skins"[10] that clothe the soul. They correspond to the four elements.

The etheric body, or memory body, is the highest vibrating of the four lower bodies and the natural envelope of the soul. The etheric body corresponds to the fire element. Within this etheric envelope, or sheath, God has placed the blueprint of the soul identity, the blueprint that will manifest as consciousness, as mind, as emotion and as the physical matrix itself.

The etheric body has two compartments. The higher etheric body contains the pristine light of our original divine plan and the record of all good that we have ever outpictured that has accrued to our causal body. It relates to the superconscious mind. The lower etheric contains the subconscious records and patterns of all that we have experienced in the Matter universe.

The two etheric bodies contain the recordings in man's being of his heaven and his earth—of the perfection of the soul's origin in God, his heaven-world, and of what he has made of his soul and his consciousness through his many experiences in his incarnations in time and space.

The mental body corresponds to the air element. This body is intended to be the vehicle of the mind of God and the mind of the Christ and the Buddha, but instead, we have taken that precious energy given to us each day and stamped upon it our version of mind, which has become the carnal mind, or the intellect. We have used the mental body to be a receptacle of worldly knowledge alone instead of the knowledge of both this world and the next.

In most of mankind, the mental body has come to be a very limited vehicle, when it could be the instrument of the fullness of the mind of God that was manifest in Jesus Christ and Gautama Buddha.

The purpose of the desire body (also called the feeling body) is to express the desire of God. God desires simply to be God. God desiring to be God ought to be the experience of our meditation and our communion. The feeling body is the body of energy-in-motion, or e-motion, corresponding to the water element.

Through this body we are intended to experience the intense feelings of God as love, as truth, as kindness, as compassion, as purity, and so forth. But instead, so many people today have used the emotional body to record the feelings of anger and pride, jealousy and revenge, hatred and intense fear and anxiety.

Finally, we have the physical body, ordained by God to be the vehicle for the soul and spirit. Although our physical body is intended to be the temple of the Holy Spirit, the temple of the living God, many have allowed all manner of perversions and impurities to enter the temple—everything from the impurities we find in our food to the darkness of impurity that is reflected from the mental and feeling worlds. The invasion of the body temple has become very great, and many are subject to unseen forces. In the time of Jesus, it was seen as demon possession.

These four lower bodies form the four sides of our great pyramid of life. They are the lines of demarcation that separate us from the mass consciousness. When we have an identity that is clearly defined in God, we can retain the uniqueness of the self in God. When our individuality is not clearly defined, then we tend to merge with every type of vibration, seen and unseen—like a jellyfish floating in the sea of the mass consciousness.

The four lower bodies are interpenetrating sheaths of consciousness. They can be likened to four colanders, stacked one on top of another. When the holes are correctly aligned, water can flow easily through all four colanders. But when the holes in the colanders do not line up, the holes are blocked and water cannot flow through. Similarly, when the four lower bodies are aligned and functioning according to their original design, the light can flow freely through them.

In many instances, the four lower bodies need to be purified and healed to be a more fitting habitation for the Spirit. The different bodies affect one another, and burdens in one body can be reflected in the other bodies. Wholeness comes through the integration of the energies of the four lower bodies, and that integration takes place through the flame in the heart.

All of God's children have a divine spark within the heart. It is their potential to become the fullness of the Higher Self, the Christ within or the Buddha within. This concept of the light within is at the heart of the major religions, East and West. Through this divine spark we have the potential to return to God, as Jesus did.

Your Soul and Your Spirit

Your lower self consists of your soul and your spirit. Yes, you have a soul and a spirit, and the two are not the same.

Your Spirit (with an uppercase "S") is the masculine aspect of God—God the Father. It also represents the plane of the I AM Presence. Your spirit (with a lowercase "s") is the distilled essence of your self. It is the pervading and predominating presence by which you are known. It is defined as the animating, or vital, principle of your life that you take with you throughout all your soul's incarnations. It determines your energy and what kind of person you are. Your spirit is the overriding vibration that is reflected in your character—the essence of who you are.

The soul is the nonpermanent aspect of being that is evolving through time and space. It is possible for the soul to be lost. It is also possible for the soul to be made permanent through the ritual of the return to God, called the ascension.

The soul is the feminine potential of man in polarity with the masculine Spirit, and thus is often referred to as "she." The soul is also known as the inner child. The inner child is extremely sensitive and has a depth of understanding and awareness at a "soul" level of what is going on in our world. The soul needs the guidance and comfort of the inner loving adult, or the Higher Self.

The Gift of Free Will

A universal law that affects us daily is the law of free will. Earth is a schoolroom. We are here to learn our lessons and graduate from this schoolroom. And in order to learn the lessons, God gave us free will here on earth.

Free will is one of the greatest gifts of the

universe. In effect, God said to us, "I am giving you free will in the entire material universe. Do what you will. If you want help, you must call to me, because I have guaranteed to you and vouch-safed to you free will in everything that you do." This earth, this physical plane is our place. And what happens in it is up to you and me.

God has given us two things: free will and planet Earth. He will not take back that free will by entering in to do for us those things that we are ordained to do. If we want God to intervene on earth, we who are in physical embodiment must speak up and authorize the heaven-world to enter in. Our call or request for help compels the angels and masters to answer from their realm of light.

God will not coerce us or force us in any way, because the joy of free will is truly the joy of cosmos, and that joy is the motor of life. Because we have free will, we can decide to do or not to do, to be or not to be. God is a loving parent, and the gift of free will is the great love of God for us. We can walk in the dignity of our right decisions and learn the consequences of our wrong ones. We can undo the wrong deci-sions and replace them with the right ones as

God guides us and as we learn from the results of our decisions.

The Equation of Karma

Most of us are here on earth because we have a mission to fulfill as well as unfinished business and debts to life. The principles of karma and reincarnation help us to understand our place in the world and give us insights into the mission that is our unique offering to the world.

Karma is a word we hear a lot these days, but few really understand how karma works, and even fewer know what to do about it. Many people think it means fate, something inevitable, and so it does. But karma is more than fate and more than the inevitable.

Karma comes from the Sanskrit word for "deed." The Hindu definition is a mental or physical action and its consequences. In the Buddhist sense, karma is defined as the universal law of cause and effect.

It is said, "What goes around, comes around." As we sow, so shall we reap. Karma is the causes we have set in motion and the effects we will reap from those causes. Our thoughts, feelings, words and actions from the past determine the life that we lead now. What we think, feel, speak and do sends out ripples into the world of form. The good or the not so good that we have set in motion from the past returns to us.

In the West, we find the law of karma is set forth throughout the Bible. The apostle Paul makes clear what our Lord taught him and what he learned from life:

> Every man shall bear his own burden.... Be not deceived; God is not mocked: for whatsoever a man soweth, that shall he also reap.
>
> For he that soweth to his flesh shall of the flesh reap corruption; but he that soweth to the Spirit shall of the Spirit reap life everlasting.
>
> And let us not be weary in well doing: for in due season we shall reap, if we faint not.
>
> As we have therefore opportunity, let us do good unto all men.[11]

Paul is telling us to make right choices in life. If we send out positive thoughts and feelings, actions and words, the same will return to us. Similarly, in time our unkind words and harmful behavior return as the negative energy cycles back to us to be balanced. The choices we make, the words we speak, our thoughts, feelings and actions affect the course of our lives and the lives of those with whom we come in contact. Decisions we have made in the past affect our present and our future. Each of us is reaping today the karma of the decisions of yesterday.

Since it is often not possible to reap all of our harvests in one lifetime, the law of karma is fulfilled through the corollary law of reincarnation. Reincarnation is God's mercy that allows us to reap the harvest of our past sowings here on earth instead of consigning us prematurely to "heaven" or "hell," when we are ready for neither and we still have things to do on earth.

In other words, God allows us to reembody to make amends for past mistakes. The outworking of the Law is very exact. We may be placed in a position whereby we might serve those whom we have wronged in past lives. And God returns to embodiment those whose opportunity to fulfill their destiny in life may have been impaired or cut short.

Karma predestines us, but our exercise of

free will allows us to break the shackles of our karma—within parameters. Reincarnation gives us the opportunity to learn the lessons that our returning karma, good and bad, teaches us with its exacting discipline. Then, free will allows us to choose to capitalize on our harvest of talents and good works and to pay the debt for, or "balance," our misuses of God's light, energy and consciousness. We make good karma and balance negative karma by serving and helping others; by sending out love, peace and compassion; by right action and right speech as the precepts of the Buddha; and by standing for truth and defending life whenever we can.

At the end of life, we will review all the actions of that life and the effects of our thoughts, words and deeds. Those who have had a preview of this life review through the near-death experience tell us that we will experience events, not just as an observer but as the one who is on the receiving end of that which we project into the world.

In Dannion Brinkley's life review, he met a being of light who said, "We are all a link in the great chain of humanity. What you do has an effect on the other links in that chain."[12]

KEYS TO THE KINGDOM

Dannion was given a period of time to reflect on how much love he had given to others and how much love he had taken. He could hear the message of the loving being: "Humans are powerful spiritual beings meant to create good on earth. This good isn't usually accomplished in bold actions, but in singular acts of kindness between people. It's the little things that count, because they are more spontaneous and show who you really are."

Dannion felt elated because he now knew the simple secret: "The amount of love and good feelings you have at the end of your life is equal to the amount of love and good feelings you put into your life. It was just that simple!"[13]

The Ascension: Reunion with God

The purpose of our soul's evolution in earth's schoolroom is to learn the lessons of life and fulfill all that we were meant to do here. Day by day we can put on more of the Christ consciousness, becoming more of that Self in manifestation.

The culmination of the path of Christhood is the ascension, a spiritual acceleration of consciousness that takes place at the natural conclusion of one's final lifetime on earth. Through the ascension, the soul merges with the Christ Self and returns to the Father-Mother God, free from the round of karma and rebirth.

The ascension comes at the conclusion of lifetimes of the soul's service to life. The prerequisites for this graduation from earth's schoolroom are: (1) The soul must become one with her Christ Self; (2) She must balance at least 51 percent of her karma; and (3) She must fulfill her mission on earth according to her divine plan.

It is possible for the soul, walking with God, to truly embody the flame, the light and the consciousness of her Real Self long before she is called home in the ritual of the ascension; but not until the hour of her ascension is she fused to the I AM Presence, one forevermore.

When the alchemical marriage of the soul to the Holy Christ Self is fully accomplished, the Holy Spirit will come to the soul, who may hear the approbation of the Father: "This is my beloved Son in whom I am well pleased,"[14] testifying that the son of man has become the sacred vessel of the Son of God.

Through the ascension, the soul becomes

the incorruptible one. Henceforth to be known as an ascended master, the soul receives the crown of everlasting life. This is the consummate goal of life, greatly to be desired.

CHAPTER 3
YOU ARE A SPIRITUAL BEING

*W*e all came into life with things that we have to do. For many of us, it is unfinished business from past lives. Every person has a divine plan. Every family, every community, even our nation and the earth itself has a divine plan, a way that things are supposed to be. And that divine plan is often very different from how things are now.

A Little Excess Baggage

The problem we have to deal with if we are to emerge from earth's schoolroom as an integrated personality in God is this: During our stay on this planet, our spiritual pores have become clogged with a lot of human karma and astral effluvia (i.e., the dust and debris of the mis-qualified energy of the centuries). In addition, each of us is carrying a percentage of the total planetary karma in our four lower bodies.

As we have misqualified God's pure life-stream perpetually flowing from our I AM Presence for our use here below, it has accumulated in the subconscious as rings on our tree of life and in the collective unconscious of the race. Like it or not, we *are* bearing one another's karmic burden, simply because we are a part of this evolution. And that, too, is our karma!

A graphic representation of how negative energy can accumulate was shown in the 1989 comedy *Ghostbusters II*. At the beginning of the film, the "ghostbusters" discover a river of pink-orange slime flowing in an abandoned Manhattan subway tunnel. They determine that the slime is the materialization of negative human emotions—hate, violence and anger. The slime begins to grow and multiply, gathering momentum in response to the population's continued output of negative energy. It starts pushing up through sidewalks, threatening to envelop the city and inaugurate a "season of evil." It can be counteracted only by positive energy—peace, love and good feelings.

In order to galvanize the positive energy of

New Yorkers, the ghostbusters positively charge the Statue of Liberty, which comes to life and wades into Manhattan. People come out in the streets and cheer. The slime is finally overcome when the crowd sings "Auld Lang Syne."

(Interestingly, the Goddess of Liberty is a great spiritual being whose retreat, the Temple of the Sun, is located in the etheric octave over Manhattan. Her retreat, once physical, was withdrawn into the etheric octave at the time of the sinking of the ancient continent of Atlantis.)

Although we don't take the movie too seriously, *Ghostbusters II* does illustrate what those who are sensitive have always known: the negative energy we put out attracts more of its kind and by and by returns to overtake us unless we seek and find resolution. Sooner or later the astral slime spills over into the physical plane— and the mist becomes the crystal.

Your Seven Energy Centers

Within our body are seven primary energy centers called *chakras* (a Sanskrit term meaning "wheel" or "disc"). The chakras are internal step-down transformers that regulate the flow of God's energy according to the needs of the four lower bodies. The seven major chakras are positioned along the spinal column from the base of the spine to the crown. They correspond to the organs in the physical body and the different groups of nerve centers.

You can think of a chakra as a sending and receiving station for energy. The chakras are not static points of light. They are dynamic energy centers that constantly take in, store and send out spiritual energy and light. The life energy, or *prana*, flows through the body along a network of threadlike nerve channels that correspond to the meridians used in acupuncture and other healing techniques.

The chakras go through an evolutionary process as we develop spiritually. They range from small and dormant to fully awakened where they emit much light. These centers can look different in different people, depending on their past and present use of energy and the diverse stages of spiritual development. The correct care and use of these energy centers leads to greater vitality in our physical body as well as the three finer bodies.

Just as you breathe in and out through your throat, so all of the chakras are taking in and giving forth the energies of God according to the frequency assigned to each specific chakra. As light streams forth from your chakras, it forms a radiating energy field (aura) that penetrates and extends beyond the boundaries of your physical form. You can send light to the planet through these seven centers of being.

The size of your auric forcefield is directly related to your mastery of the seven energy centers, particularly the heart center. The more self-mastery you have, the larger your aura, and hence, the more effect you have on the world. A great adept or spiritual being or saint might have an aura that would encompass an entire city.

Remember Jesus' parable of the five foolish virgins and the five wise virgins? It is really a lesson in keeping the light in our chakras. The wise virgins are the ones who kept oil in their lamps. In a spiritual sense, their lamps were their chakras, their spiritual energy centers. Our chakras are meant to be full of light, and the wise virgins kept their lamps full of oil—their spiritual centers were full of light.

The foolish virgins wasted and squandered the light of their chakras, and they had no oil left in their lamps. The bridegroom is the Christ, the

Higher Self, the master, or the teacher. When the bridegroom came, the foolish virgins could not enter because they didn't have the light in their aura. The lesson of the parable is this: if we have light in our chakras, we are more able to receive the Higher Self, the angels and the masters.

The chakras are called lotuses because when viewed from the spiritual realm, they appear as a flower unfolding. Each chakra has a certain number of petals that establishes its frequency or vibration. The prophet Ezekiel described the chakras as wheels within wheels.

The charts on pages 67-68 show the seven chakras, the color and number of petals of each chakra, and the qualities of the energy that can be experienced in each chakra.

You may have noticed that some schools of thought have described different colors for the chakras. The ascended masters have released to their messengers the pure colors, as they would appear in the chakras at the highest levels of the purified etheric body. However, at lower levels of being they may well look different, especially when the aura is not purified. Some clairvoyants who have put forth their version of the colors have seen the condition of the chakras in the unpurified state of the human consciousness.

When the chakras are purified and balanced in the plus and minus factors, the yang and the yin of the whirling T'ai Chi, they emit the pure colors of the seven rays of the causal body, the spheres within spheres surrounding the I AM Presence. (See the Chart of Your Divine Self, p. 38.)

Ideally the chakra should vibrate on the same wavelength as the corresponding sphere of the causal body—"as Above, so below." Therefore, there are the seven rays, the seven spheres and the seven chakras. Let us take each chakra in turn from the top to the bottom:

The crown chakra is the point of thinking and cogitation. It is the light, or halo, seen around the head area in the aura of the saints. In the East, the crown chakra is called the thousand-petalled lotus. When you study, you are centered in your mind and your energy is centered in this chakra. Your brain is intended to be a vessel for the same mind that was in Christ Jesus, and you are intended to experience the mind of God.

The third eye is located at the center of the brow. Here we experience God as concentration as we focus and visualize through the mind's eye. This is the chakra connected with vision, both spiritual and physical. Through it we are intended to see God's creation as he sees it—pure and perfect. In this chakra we can use the science of the immaculate concept to bring forth the best in ourselves and in others.

The throat chakra is our power center. The power of speech and the spoken Word give us the power to create, preserve and destroy. Our voice and our words speak volumes and can influence people for good or ill. As we speak to others, we can bless them or curse them, elevate or belittle them. We can do all things with the spoken Word because it is the gift of God and the place where we experience God as power.

In the heart chakra, in the center of the chest, we experience God as love. The heart's love is experienced each and every time we love one another as God has loved us. Divine love is a disciplined path that is not easy but is well worth the effort.

The solar-plexus chakra is intended to be the place of peace. Jesus was the Prince of Peace and had complete mastery in this chakra. We are intended to have the same mastery. Located just

THE SEVEN CHAKRAS AND THE SEVEN RAYS

Chakra	Ray	Color	Petals
Crown	2	golden yellow	972
Third Eye	5	emerald green	96
Throat	1	blue	16
Heart	3	pink	12
Solar Plexus	6	purple and gold flecked with ruby	10
Seat of the Soul	7	violet	6
Base of the Spine	4	white	4

USES AND MISUSES OF THE CHAKRAS

Chakra	Positive Expression	Unbalanced Expression
Crown	illumination, wisdom, self-knowledge, understanding	intellectual and spiritual pride, intellectualism, vanity, narrow-mindedness, ignorance
Third Eye	healing, truth, vision, abundance, constancy	falsehood, lack of vision, mental criticism, lack of clarity
Throat	power, will, faith, protection, courage	control, condemnation, idle chatter, gossip, cowardice, doubt
Heart	love, compassion, beauty, selflessness	hatred, dislike, selfishness, self-pity, human sympathy, negligence
Solar Plexus	peace, brotherhood, service, balance	anger, agitation, fanaticism, fear, anxiety, passivity, overindulgence
Seat of the Soul	freedom, mercy, forgiveness, justice, alchemy	lack of forgiveness, justice or mercy; intolerance, disregard for others
Base of the Spine	purity, hope, joy, self-discipline	discouragement, hopelessness, impurity, chaos

above the navel, this chakra is called the place of the sun. It is the place from which rivers of living water should flow, as Jesus said.[15] In each chakra, we experience the antithesis of God as well as the fullness of God, and the solar plexus is the point where we experience our emotions, both good and bad. When we are upset or angry or nervous, we feel it in the pit of the stomach.

The seat-of-the-soul chakra is where our soul is anchored in our body. This chakra contains the pattern of our identity. It governs the creation of the genes and what we pass on in procreation as well as in all our creations in life.

This is the place where we get our "gut" feelings, or intuition. When we sense danger or that we need to leave or to go to a certain place or take a certain action, we often experience this "soul direction" at the seat-of-the-soul chakra.

Another name for the soul is the psyche. Hence, those who are psychic are those who are sensitive to the communications of the soul. Unfortunately, many who are psychic are often attuned to the lower vibrations instead of the higher destiny of the soul and its origin in Spirit.

The base-of-the-spine chakra is the lowest point to which the light descends in the body,

Centers of Light in the Body of Man

the location of the white fire, the life-force. It is the light of the Divine Mother. Here we experience the power of creation and the ability to procreate. We are intended to raise the light of this chakra through all of the chakras for their nourishment.

The seven chakras can be thought of as seven ways of experiencing God in your life. Each of those seven experiences gives an intimation of the seven spheres of the causal body—the many mansions of our Father's house.[16]

There are specific musical instruments and gemstones that amplify the action of each chakra. The seven major world religions also correspond to the seven chakras. These correspondences are listed in the chart on page 74 along with the anchor point for each chakra in the physical body.

The Heart Chakra

The heart chakra is the most important of our seven spiritual centers. The other chakras are defined by their location above and below the heart. There are three chakras above the heart and three below.

The heart is the hub of life physically and spiritually. The heart chakra is the center through which we give and receive love. It is located within the chest cavity and is often depicted as the rose of the heart. The color of

The Heart Chakra

love is the beautiful pink of the rose—the shades ranging from a deep ruby-pink to a delicate rose-pink color.

The Secret Chamber of the Heart

Within the heart chakra is another smaller spiritual center called the secret chamber of the heart. Jesus spoke of entering the secret chamber of the heart when he said: "When thou prayest, enter into thy closet, and when thou hast shut thy door, pray to thy Father which is in secret; and thy Father which seeth in secret shall reward thee openly."[17]

When we go into our closet to pray, we are actually entering into another dimension of consciousness. We can enter into the closet of the heart and close the door on the outside world. The mystics understood this chamber within the heart. Teresa of Avila called it the interior castle—it was the place where she would commune with her beloved Jesus. The secret chamber of the heart is where the soul receives the mysteries of life.

The only way we can get into the secret chamber is through love—we must have passed the tests and the initiations of the love of the heart. As we pass through the love chakra, we come to, as it were, a temple door at the rear. We go through the door, and we enter the secret chamber, and there seated upon the throne is the Inner Christ.

In Hindu tradition, the devotee visualizes a jeweled island in the heart. On this island, he sees before him a beautiful altar where he worships his teacher in deep meditation. You can think of the secret chamber of your heart as your

private medita-
tion room. It is
the place where
you can com-
mune with the
Inner Christ, your
Holy Christ Self,
the still small
voice that speaks
to you within
your heart.

The Secret Chamber of the Heart

73

THE SEVEN CHAKRAS AND THEIR CORRESPONDENCES

Chakra	Gemstone	Musical Instrument	Anchor Point in the Physical Body	Spiritual Tradition
Crown	yellow diamond, yellow sapphire, topaz	strings	pineal	Buddhism
Third Eye	emerald, diamond, jade, quartz crystal	piano	pituitary	Confucianism
Throat	diamond, sapphire, star sapphire, lapis lazuli	brass	thyroid	Judaism
Heart	ruby, diamond, garnet rose quartz, pink beryl	harp	heart	Christianity
Solar Plexus	topaz, ruby, alexandrite diamond with pearl	organ	pancreas	Islam
Seat of the Soul	amethyst, diamond, aquamarine	woodwinds	ovaries or prostate	Taoism
Base of the Spine	diamond, pearl zircon, quartz crystal	drum, tabla	genitals	Hinduism

The Threefold Flame of the Heart

Within the secret chamber of the heart is a flame that blazes upon the altar. It is called the threefold flame. This flame is the spark of life projected from the Higher Self and anchored in the heart chakra. It is the gift of life to us from our Father-Mother God.

The threefold flame has three petals—blue, yellow and pink. The blue (on your left), the yellow (in the center) and the pink (on your right) correspond to the primary attributes of power, wisdom and love, respectively. These flames arise from a sphere of white light that is the flame of the Mother.

The flames of power, wisdom and love—or faith, hope and charity—are the Trinity within you. The power (of the Father), the wisdom (of the Son) and the love (of the Holy Spirit) are all anchored in the threefold flame.

The threefold flame within the human heart pulsates to liberate the divine blueprint of life into the bodily form. This flame (one-sixteenth of an inch in height) is the divine spark, the potential of your divinity. It is the gift of life of the Creator to the creation. Truly this threefold flame is the light which lighteth every man and woman that cometh into the world.[18]

The consciousness of the Son of God is centered in this flame, which is also called the Holy Christ Flame. "For God so loved the world, that he gave his only begotten Son"—to live

within us as the flame within the heart.[19]

This flame is the individualization of the God flame whereby the Word is "made flesh"[20] in you, enabling you to behold the glory of the Lord of all within your members. The flame that burns within your heart is the seat of cos-

The Threefold Flame

mic consciousness. It is your link to Reality, to Being and to life eternal.

The heart flame needs to be tended, just as the heart chakra needs to be developed to give and receive more love. The three plumes of this flame are also intended to be expanded, accelerated and balanced to the same height. If they are not, a lack of development in one flame can actually impair the expansion of the other flames.

For example, if you have a large blue flame of power but little development on the pink (love) and yellow (wisdom), you might tend to be dictatorial or tyrannical, without having the balance of love and wisdom to temper the power. Before you can be given any more stature to the blue flame, you are required to develop more love and wisdom, so that you can use the power wisely and lovingly. The tests that come your way will be designed to assist you to develop these plumes so that they are not out of balance. In fact, if you do not attempt to develop your pink and yellow plumes, your larger blue plume may *shrink* in size as a means to bring balance.

As you serve harmoniously as the vessel of your higher consciousness, through the work of your heart, head and hand balanced in the flow of love, wisdom and power, there can come about a corresponding balance in the threefold flame.

Guarding the Heart

The heart is a very delicate chalice for the sacred flame of God that burns within it, and the adepts advise us to guard the heart. We want to protect the chalice of the heart against the shock waves that come from discord, stress, or our own moods and emotions. It is important to pray for the protection of the heart, and when you pray and meditate, it is always wise to call to your Higher Self and the angels for protection.

The Holy Spirit

Mankind have been given the teachings of God in stages, in cycles. For two thousand years we have been given an understanding of God as the Son, and we have come to understand God through the person of Jesus. Prior to that, Moses, as the very personal representative of the Law, revealed God as Father, as the Lawgiver.

In this two-thousand-year period that is beginning, we are finding a tremendous awakening to the energies of the Holy Spirit. People are calling upon the name of the Lord, and they are asking God to infill them with that Holy Spirit. This completes the Trinity realized in the consciousness of mankind over several thousand years.

The Holy Spirit is the third aspect of the Trinity. It is the feeling attribute that energizes and motivates thought into action. It enables us to apply our knowledge and precipitate it into action, bringing our projects to fruition. The Holy Spirit is often portrayed as a pink color, embodying love, compassion and comfort.

The Holy Spirit is often depicted symbolically as a dove, as seen in the Chart of Your Divine Self. (See page 38.) The gentle ministrations of the dove of the Holy Spirit descend from on high, releasing the God-qualities of all the rays. Prana is the essence of the Holy Spirit that we take in by the sacred fire breath through the chakras to nourish the four lower bodies.

The Holy Spirit is the Comforter that Jesus promised he would send us to bring all things to our remembrance.[21] Thus, the teachings of Jesus that were not preserved in the scriptures, but have been lost for these 2,000 years, are being brought forth again in the age of Aquarius, the age of the Holy Spirit. These are the inner mysteries that Jesus gave to his disciples in the Upper Room.

The descent of the Holy Ghost was promised by Jesus to his disciples when he said, "Tarry ye in the city of Jerusalem, until ye be endued with power from on high."[22] This took place on

Pentecost, when the Holy Spirit, as a rushing mighty wind, filled all the house where they were staying.

The Holy Spirit brings great enlightenment, teaching us those things we need to know, and we are all intended to become agents of the Holy Spirit. Messengers of God are anointed by the Holy Spirit, and their teachings are delivered through the power of the Holy Spirit.

The Maha Chohan is the representative of the Holy Spirit to planet Earth, conveying the energies of the Holy Spirit to the human octave. Maha Chohan means "Great Lord." Serving on the eighth ray of integration, he is teacher and guru to the seven chohans. He is master of all the rays, because the Holy Spirit contains all the rays.

The Hindus called the Holy Spirit the Destroyer, Shiva—the one who breaks down the misqualified energies, or the misuses of life that we have brought forth by our misuse of free will. For example, we have free will to qualify God's energy as love or as hatred. If we have qualified it as hatred, that energy rests with us and remains as part of our consciousness until we transmute it by love. The power of the Holy Spirit to transmute hatred into love manifests by the dispensation of the violet flame.

The Holy Spirit is the omnipresence of God, the cloven tongues of fire focusing energies of the Father-Mother God. This spirit is also called the sacred fire—it is the energy of life that infuses a cosmos. This all-consuming love, when invoked in the planes of Matter, binds the forces of evil and transmutes the cause and effect of man's miscreations, thus delivering him from the prison house of karma and its dark denizens. The exorcism of foul spirits and unclean entities is accomplished by the sacred fire of the Holy Spirit in the name of Christ and the I AM THAT I AM.

The Maha Chohan

There are nine gifts of the Holy Spirit, powers conveyed to the Lord's servants to bind death and hell and work His works on earth. As we apprentice ourselves under the seven chohans, we can also qualify to receive these gifts. Saint Paul describes them in his Epistle to the Corinthians:

For to one is given by the Spirit the word of wisdom; to another the word of knowledge by the same Spirit; to another faith by the same Spirit; to another the gifts of healing by the same Spirit; to another the working of miracles; to another prophecy; to another discerning of spirits; to another divers kinds of tongues; to another the interpretation of tongues: but all these worketh that one and the selfsame Spirit, dividing to every man severally as he will.[23]

The Flame of the Mother

God is the androgynous whole, and we can speak to God as Father and we can speak to God as Mother. The Chinese have the magnificent symbol of the T'ai Chi representing the masculine and the feminine aspects of the Whole.

All things come from the circle of energy of the plus and the minus, the Alpha, the Omega. This energy as God is present within us all, and as we meditate upon this energy, we can feel the wholeness of the presence of the Father-Mother God.

The Aquarian age is the age of the Holy

Spirit, and it is also destined to be the age of the rise of the feminine principle—of God as Mother. We see this reflected in women all over the world coming into their own after thousands of years of not realizing their true identity in a world dominated by the masculine ray. Our devotion to God as Mother will create the balance in the individual and in our civilization that is necessary for the alchemy of self-transformation.

Ancient civilizations have risen and fallen by the use or misuse of the light of the Mother flame. The culture of the Mother is the culture that existed on the golden-age civilizations of Lemuria and Atlantis. Now is the moment when we must work to restore the true culture of America and all nations, which is the culture of the Mother of the World.

The Mother of the World is the object of the adoration and meditation of the Buddhas and the Christs. She is seeking her children and desires to rescue them from the burdens that beset them. The principle of the Mother flame is exemplified and personified by the ascended lady masters of heaven, great beings such as Mother Mary, the divine mother of the West, and Kuan Yin, the compassionate saviouress of the East.

In each one of us individually, the Mother light is anchored in the base-of-the-spine

chakra, the fount of the Mother, and the Father energy is focused in the crown chakra. As the two unite in the heart chakra, the Father and Mother principles within us give birth to the Christ consciousness.

The T'ai Chi

One means to gently raise the light of the Mother from the base to the crown is through the giving of the rosary. The rosary is one means of our soul's meditation upon God as we rise to the level of the Christ within the heart.

In the New Age Rosary that Mother Mary has given to us, we alternate the prayer of the Hail Mary with contemplation of the life and experiences of Jesus as we listen to readings from the Bible. We meditate alternately upon Mary the Mother, the focal point of our own incarnation of the Motherhood of God, and upon Jesus Christ for our realization of the fullness of that Divine Sonship within us. Through the Mother and the Son we reach the Father, and in the Father we are reborn according to his immaculate design. The rosary, then, is for the balance of the masculine and feminine polarity of being. In her appearances at Fátima, Mother Mary has outlined her plan to bring peace to the world and an end to war through daily recitation of the rosary.

There are many stories of miracles people have experienced through the rosary. One notable example is that of eight men who survived Hiroshima. When an atomic bomb destroyed the city in 1945, eight men living near the blinding center of the nuclear flash miraculously survived the searing hurricane of blast and radiation while everyone within a mile radius perished immediately and others residing further afield died later from the lethal effects of radiation. For over thirty years, some two hundred scientists have examined these eight men, trying in vain to determine what could have preserved them from incineration.

One of the survivors, Father H. Shiffner, S.J., gave the dramatic answer on TV in America when he said, "In that house the rosary was prayed every day. In that house we were living the message of Fátima."[24]

Mary has explained that the "Hail Mary" is actually "Hail Ma-Ray," or "Mother Ray." It is a universal adoration of God as Mother in the many beings of light who embody that Mother

Kuan Yin and Mother Mary

flame. It is also the prayer for the expansion and raising of the Mother light within us.

Mary has asked that as we pray the Hail Mary in this age, we no longer contemplate death as our destination, but that we affirm our victory over death in the resurrection and ascension. Therefore she has asked us to pray:

Hail, Mary, full of grace,
   the Lord is with thee.
Blessed art thou among women
   and blessed is the fruit
   of thy womb, Jesus.

Holy Mary, Mother of God,
Pray for us, sons and daughters of God,
Now and at the hour of our victory
Over sin, disease and death.

Keeping the Flame of Life

Through the ages, members of the Great White Brotherhood have come forth to sponsor uplift movements and to assist the lifewaves of earth in every aspect of their evolution. Great artists, inventors, scientists, statesmen and religious leaders—as well as the pure in heart from every walk of life—have been overshadowed by various members of this spiritual hierarchy.

Saint Germain—patron of the United States of America and hierarch of the Aquarian age—has once again stepped forth to sponsor an outer activity of the Great White Brotherhood. He founded the Keepers of the Flame Fraternity for those who want to serve with members of the heavenly hierarchy. The purpose is to join masters ascended with striving souls on earth to form a united action for the salvation of those of the light in this age. The Keepers of the Flame Fraternity provides the counterpart here below to the Great White Brotherhood Above.

Saint Germain

Keepers of the Flame pledge their support to the ascended master Saint Germain to assist him in the publication and distribution of the true teachings of Jesus Christ. As Keepers of the Flame give their support to Saint Germain, he in turn sponsors their personal path of initiation, releasing instruction in cosmic law, which, when applied, leads to self-mastery.

The Keepers of the Flame Lessons, supplemented by the *Pearls of Wisdom* and other publications, set forth the teachings of the ascended masters that enable the devotee to make the transition in consciousness from any religion or no religion to self-conscious awareness in God. They open the way to a true understanding of the laws of God affecting his life and world.

Keepers of the Flame agree to perform certain spiritual work each day for the keeping of the flame of life on behalf of all mankind. In many ways it is an outer sign of inner commitment to keep the flame until others are able to keep the flame for themselves.

To join the Keepers of the Flame Fraternity is an outer commitment to Saint Germain. It is a commitment to keep the flame of life for one's self and for the world.

CHAPTER 4
TOOLS FOR TRANSFORMATION

*T*he masters have given us powerful tools for transformation and change in our lives and in the life of the world around us. One of the most important of these is prayer.

The Power of Prayer

Prayer is the language of the soul. In its essence, it is simply conversation with God, communion with him and listening to his answers. And we need prayer as never before. No matter what their faith, everyone's prayers count in heaven, especially the prayers of children and mothers.

One recent poll has said that 82 percent of Americans believe in the healing power of personal prayer.[25] No one really knows scientifically how or why prayer is so effective in healing.

But an increasing number of studies suggest what people have known intuitively for thousands of years—that prayer really works. It almost doesn't matter what form the prayer takes; the simple act of expressing desire to a Higher Power brings results.

Even science and medicine are coming around to this idea. One well-known study found that coronary patients at San Francisco General Hospital who were prayed for did better than those who did not receive prayers. The patients who received prayers required fewer antibiotics and were less likely to develop certain complications than those who were not in the prayer group. One doctor said of the coronary study, "Maybe we doctors ought to be writing on our order sheets, 'Pray three times a day.' If it works, it works."[26]

Another study, at Dartmouth-Hitchcock Medical Center, examined how patients' own prayers affected their recovery from open-heart surgery. This 1995 study found that patients who said they drew comfort and strength from religious faith, which presumably included prayer, were three times more likely to survive in the six months following surgery than "non-religious" patients.

The Bible tells us, "The effectual fervent prayer of a righteous man availeth much."[27] Notice those three qualifying words—fervent, effectual and righteous. Fervent means with your heart and with your devotion—not weak or passive. Effectual means effective, and there is indeed a science and an art to the practice of prayer. And the prayer of a righteous man, a man or a woman who is right with God, does bring great fruit.

If you are unsure how to pray, just think of prayer as conversation with God. Pray and talk to God as your dearest friend. Tell him what you want him to know and what you want him to do for you, your family, community and nation. Ask him for gifts and graces. And don't be attached to the outcome. Simply say, "Not my will but thine be done."

All of the saints have understood the holy power and simplicity of prayer. Saint Thérèse of Lisieux said it beautifully:

"I have not the courage to look through books for beautiful prayers. I only get a headache because of their number, and besides, one is more lovely than another. Unable therefore to say them all, and lost in choice, I do as children who have not learnt to read—I simply tell Our Lord all that I want and He always understands."[28]

All of us would do well to pray very specifically and tell God what it is we wish to see happen in our lives—and also in the world. We can ask him to forestall events such as terrorism, war or economic instability. Before the mist of prophecy becomes the crystal, it can be turned back, if it be in accordance with the will of God.

The Creative Power of Sound

Mystics have known for thousands of years that sound holds the key to the creation of the universe. Prayer and mantra can create spiritual and material change in our lives. When spoken out loud, prayer can unlock the dynamic energy of Spirit.

The creative power of sound is beautifully illustrated in this example from the lives of one group of Benedictine monks. In 1967 Alfred Tomatis, a French physician, psychologist and ear specialist, studied how chanting affected the Benedictine monks. For hundreds of years they had kept a rigorous schedule, sleeping only a few hours a night and chanting from six to eight hours a day. When a new abbot changed the schedule and cut out the chanting, the monks became tired and lethargic. The more sleep they got, the more tired they seemed to become.

Tomatis was called to find out what was wrong with them. He believed that chanting (and listening to certain kinds of music) served a special purpose—energizing the brain and the body. He said the monks "had been chanting in order to 'charge' themselves."[29] He reintroduced chanting, along with a program of listening to stimulating sounds, and the monks soon found the energy to return to their normal schedule. Whether the monks knew it or not, they had discovered the power of sound, especially spoken or chanted prayer.

In the East, people repeat mantras over and over many times a day. But in the West, we are not always accustomed to this practice of repeating prayers. Each time you repeat a prayer, you strengthen the power of the request by qualifying it with more and more of God's light and energy. You also begin to enter into a state of oneness with God.

Both mystics and scientists have demonstrated

the benefits of repetitive prayer. From members of the Eastern Orthodox Church to medieval monks, mystics East and West have reported extraordinary mystical experiences and a feeling of oneness with God, even entering an altered state in which the flesh is "kindled by the Spirit, so that the whole man becomes spiritual."[30]

In the early 1970s, Dr. Herbert Benson, president and founder of the Mind/Body Medical Institute at Harvard Medical School, experimented scientifically with the power of prayer. He told his subjects to sit quietly and repeat Sanskrit mantras either mentally or verbally for ten to twenty minutes, to breathe regularly and to push intruding thoughts aside as they entered their minds.

He found that those who repeated these mantras for as little as ten minutes a day experienced physiological changes: reduced heart rate, lower stress levels and slower metabolism. Those with high blood pressure found that the repetition of mantras lowered their blood pressure. He called this phenomenon "the relaxation response," which he says is the opposite of the body's fight-or-flight mechanism. Subsequent studies documented in Benson's

Timeless Healing found that repeating mantras can benefit the immune system, relieve insomnia and reduce doctor visits.

Benson found that other prayers had the same effect. Even words like *one, ocean, love* and *peace* produced the response. It appears that there is a universal principle at work here—repetitive prayer allows human beings to enter a relaxed state. And the spiritual benefits are just as important, perhaps more so. Many Buddhists and Hindus will tell you that repetition of mantras or prayers allows the mind to focus on God, just as Eastern Orthodox monks find joy, happiness and oneness with God through repetitive prayer.

The goal of entering into a higher state of consciousness, greater access to the Higher Mind and a state of oneness with God is the reason why many people repeat mantras, chants and prayers.

The Science of the Spoken Word

The prayers and affirmations in this book are most effective when given aloud as a dynamic prayer form known as "decrees." When we decree, we are commanding the flow of energy from Spirit to Matter for personal and world transformation. We are not just asking for help; we are entering into a partnership and an interactive relationship with God.

This is what God asked us to do when he said through the prophet Isaiah, "Concerning the work of my hands command ye me."[31] And we read in the Book of Job, "Thou shalt make thy prayer unto him [the Almighty], and he shall hear thee.... Thou shalt also decree a thing, and it shall be established unto thee."[32]

Decrees are a part of a system of prayer called the science of the spoken Word, which also includes songs, mantras and chants, as well as visualizations and breathing techniques. Decrees are positive affirmations that use the name of God, I AM THAT I AM. The primary purpose is to put you in contact with your Higher Self. Once you have that contact, you can draw on the power of the God within to bring you the things you need in life. You can use that spiritual energy to create positive change for yourself and the world around you.

Devotion is the key to the power of mantra and song and decree. You will find decrees and mantras at the back of this book that will assist you in many ways and that can help you find peace and greater contact with your Higher Self.

There is a mantra and decree for everyone, and any number of mantras or decrees for us all. Pick your mantra and decree, and let it be something profoundly meaningful to you, so that each time you say the words, you can feel the words happening—and more than the words happening, because somewhere inside of you there is a resonance with that particular mantra or decree. The mantra is like a grid of energy— your heart's devotion is magnified through it.

It is not the words that we speak or the length of time that we pray but the love that we put into it that will change our world and the world around us. Devotion is the way that we keep angels with us, because devotion opens the channels. Our devotion goes to God and the angels. We have opened a highway to our God, and the angels travel down that highway back to our hearts.

Saint Germain and the Violet Flame

In the Chart of Your Divine Self, you can see the lower figure enveloped in the violet flame, the light of the seventh ray. This violet energy can have profound effects on all aspects of our being—mental, emotional and even physical.

The violet flame is a spiritual energy used in the retreats in the heaven-world. It is also known as the mercy flame or the flame of forgiveness, as well as the freedom flame. This seventh-ray aspect of the Holy Spirit can be called forth through prayer and mantra.

We can use the analogy of a film in a movie projector to describe the action of the violet flame. As you use the violet transmuting flame, you are washing the imperfections and streaks from the film of life and from the lens. You purify the lens, and the film is washed and altered by master artisans, so that it can reflect the purity of the light rays passing through it.

As you change and transmute the film that is in the projector of your consciousness, you will alter the picture that is cast upon the screen of life. You can then become a manifestation of perfection, designed in the form of a son or a daughter of God. You are no longer an individual expressing temporal manifestations of imperfection, but you are a son or daughter of the Most High God as you drink in the consciousness of the eternal light that is within you.

The violet flame can be used to transmute, or change, any negative energy in our lives—the energies of hatred, anger, discord and hardness of heart. Devotees use it to transmute negative karma and to produce positive change in all areas of human endeavor, whether personal or planetary in scope.

The following is a simple mantra from the master Saint Germain, the master who introduced the violet flame to mankind:

> *I AM a being of violet fire,*
> *I AM the purity God desires.*

As you give this mantra, you can visualize this high-frequency spiritual energy of the violet flame erasing your problems, resolving burdens and liberating you from sadness or regret due to poor choices in the past.

Every day, the angels deliver to us a new little pack of karma, our assignment for the day. If we douse it with violet flame at dawn, we can transmute and soften the karma, then balance the rest in service through our job, our family and community, and whatever good works we do on that day.

Don't let your karma pile up, because you

can get burdened by it. Clean up the day's offering as it arrives, and if you can do a bit extra to clean up the rest of this life and a bit more for previous lifetimes, you will be well on your way to accelerating your consciousness.

Heart, Head and Hand Decrees

The ascended master El Morya has released a series of mantras that contain the keys to the steps and stages on the spiritual path. These "Heart, Head and Hand Decrees" commemorate Christ's mission and the steps of initiation he demonstrated in his Galilean embodiment.

Your heart, head and hands are your instruments for the Trinity of life in expression. The work of heart, head and hand in balance is intended to express the love of the Son in the heart, the wisdom of the Father in the head and the power of the Holy Spirit in action through the work of your hands. The heart receives, the head interprets and the hand of the Holy Spirit executes the design of the divine plan.

Several of these verses in the "Heart, Head and Hand Decrees" are in the form of "I AM" affirmations. Since I AM is the name of God (as he revealed it to Moses[33]), when we affirm

"I AM," we are really saying "God in me is" or "God in me is the action of...." Whatever follows—whether it be speech, prayer, mantra or decree—it is self-realized because it is the power of God's name and his Be-ness that works creative change in our lives.

El Morya

When you use the name "I AM," it's not just a positive affirmation. God is fulfilling that decree in you because you are using his name, because you are his son or daughter, and you are a joint-heir of the Christ consciousness Jesus had.

Each verse of the "Heart, Head and Hand Decrees" corresponds to a specific chakra. If you give each verse at least three times, you will have the action of the Trinity in each of the chakras.

Heart, Head and Hand (Heart Chakra)

The first mantra invites the violet flame into the heart. We have hardness of heart recorded there, an absence of forgiveness, tensions, doubts, fears. Just the very trauma of modern

103

existence in the major cities produces a burden on the heart. When the heart is cleared, it can be a chalice for the Real Self.

> Violet fire, thou love divine,
> Blaze within this heart
>   of mine!
> Thou art mercy forever true,
> Keep me always in tune
>   with you.

Now we call forth the violet flame to blaze into the entire head area from the base of the neck upwards. We desire the violet flame to pass through the mind, to clear the debris of all concepts that are not clear, truthful or founded on the science of being. The apostle wrote, "Let this mind be in you which was also in Christ Jesus."[34] The violet flame, as the agency of the Holy Spirit, is the means whereby our physical, mental and spiritual vehicles can be restored to manifest the mind of God.

> I AM light, thou Christ in me,
> Set my mind forever free;
> Violet fire, forever shine
> Deep within this mind of mine.

God who gives my daily bread,
With violet fire fill my head
Till thy radiance heavenlike
Makes my mind a mind of light.

There are secret-ray chakras in the hands and feet at the points where the body of Christ was pierced. The hands are the symbol of God in action as the Holy Spirit. All that we touch with our hands can be blessed with the Holy Spirit action of the violet flame.

I AM the hand of God in action,
Gaining victory every day;
My pure soul's great satisfaction
Is to walk the Middle Way.

Tube of Light (Secret Chamber of the Heart)

Zechariah said, "I, saith the LORD, will be unto her a wall of fire round about, and will be the glory in the midst of her."[35] The tube of light is the wall round about, and the violet fire is the glory in the midst. The tube of light is your seamless garment, descending around you like a waterfall of light, forming an armour of protection around you. It seals you from the mass consciousness and the energies of the

Crown Chakra

Third-Eye Chakra

Throat Chakra

Heart Chakra

Solar-Plexus Chakra

Seat-of-the-Soul Chakra

Base-of-the-Spine Chakra

world. As you give this decree, see yourself as the lower figure in the Chart of Your Divine Self (see page 38), standing in the violet flame and sealed in the tube of light.

Beloved I AM Presence bright,
Round me seal your tube of
    light
From ascended master flame
Called forth now in God's
    own name.
Let it keep my temple free
From all discord sent to me.

I AM calling forth violet fire
To blaze and transmute all
    desire,
Keeping on in freedom's name
Till I AM one with the violet
    flame.

Forgiveness (Seat-of-the-Soul Chakra)

Jesus' first miracle, which he demonstrated at the marriage at Cana, was the changing of the water into wine. This symbolizes his mission as a demonstration of the science of the use of God's energy, the forgiveness of the waters of the human consciousness that they might be changed into the wine of Spirit.

Forgiveness is the first step on the spiritual path. Whenever we pray or come to the altar or meditate, we must first call upon the law of forgiveness. Forgiveness is the beginning of the resolution of all problems, personal and planetary.

As you give this decree, see spheres of violet-purple-pink energy going forth to bless all mankind—all those with whom you have karma, all whom you have wronged and all who have wronged you. Do not forget to forgive yourself.

> I AM forgiveness acting here,
> Casting out all doubt and fear,
> Setting men forever free
> With wings of cosmic victory.
>
> I AM calling in full power
> For forgiveness every hour;
> To all life in every place
> I flood forth forgiving grace.

Supply (Third-Eye Chakra)

All abundance, both spiritual and material,

ultimately comes from God, the I AM Presence. We are intended to have the supply that we need to fulfill our divine plan and to assist all mankind and the planet in entering into a golden age.

Saint Germain teaches us to visualize supply as precipitated gold. Of all the elements, gold represents precipitated sunlight—the gold of the golden rule, as the golden consciousness of the mind of Christ.

Fear and doubt block supply. The violet flame is used to clear all blocks to the abundant life in all levels of our consciousness, especially fear. As you give this decree, visualize the green of the fifth ray of abundance all around you, mingling with the violet flame, and see gold coins descending into your hands.

> I AM free from fear and doubt,
> Casting want and misery out,
> Knowing now all good supply
> Ever comes from realms on high.
>
> I AM the hand of God's own fortune
> Flooding forth the treasures of light,
> Now receiving full abundance
> To supply each need of life.

Perfection (Throat Chakra)

Jesus said, "Be ye therefore perfect, even as your Father which is in heaven is perfect."[36] There is a divine plan, a perfect inner blueprint for the way our life should be lived. We visualize this as a great blue sphere that descends from our causal body into our aura. Through the law of perfection, this sphere brings alignment with the divine plan and pattern for our life.

This mantra for perfection restores the memory stored in the etheric body of the vow we made before we came into embodiment, of the mission we came to earth to fulfill.

> I AM life of God-direction,
> Blaze thy light of truth in me.
> Focus here all God's perfection,
> From all discord set me free.
>
> Make and keep me anchored ever
> In the justice of thy plan—
> I AM the Presence of perfection
> Living the life of God in man!

Transfiguration (Crown Chakra)

On the Mount of Transfiguration, Jesus, the great scientist of the Piscean age, demonstrated the law of universal energy whereby he compelled the inner nucleus of the I AM Presence to release and emit its light. He also commanded the nucleus of every physical atom of his body, billions of atoms of substance, to emit their energy in a certain degree desired. And what was the result? Scripture records that his countenance shone like lightning and his garments became glistering white.[37]

As we give this decree and call for the light of the transfiguration, we are changing our vibration, changing our consciousness. Each day we can put off our old garments of sin, self-belittlement and condemnation, and each day we can put on the robe, the inner garment, of our Christ consciousness.

> I AM changing all my garments,
> Old ones for the bright new day;
> With the sun of understanding
> I AM shining all the way.
>
> I AM light within, without;
> I AM light is all about.
> Fill me, free me, glorify me!
> Seal me, heal me, purify me!
> Until transfigured they describe me:

I AM shining like the Son,
I AM shining like the Sun!

Resurrection (Solar-Plexus Chakra)

At the point of Jesus' resurrection, he returned to the place where his body lay, the tomb of Matter, the laboratory of Matter. There was an angel at the head and an angel at the feet holding the masculine and feminine polarity of the resurrection flame. Jesus gave the command by the science of the spoken Word for the resurrection flame to enter his body, resurrecting his physical form.

The resurrection flame is a combination of the Trinity—the pink, yellow and blue. As the threefold flame is balanced and expanded, the vibration accelerates, and the three plumes begin to spin. As they do, they take on the color of the mother-of-pearl, the white light containing within it all of the hues of the rainbow.

The resurrection flame is a powerful adjunct to healing. It has the capacity to restore life to its proper functioning, rejuvenating the body and resurrecting the memory of the original divine plan.

I AM the flame of resurrection
Blazing God's pure light through me.
Now I AM raising every atom,
From every shadow I AM free.

I AM the light of God's full Presence,
I AM living ever free.
Now the flame of life eternal
Rises up to victory.

Ascension (Base-of-the-Spine Chakra)

On Bethany's hill, in the presence of 500 witnesses, the cloud of Jesus' I AM Presence "received him out of their sight"—out of their line of vision, or vibration. And so the record was left for all time that the ascension is the goal of life for every son and daughter of God.

We ascend a little each day as a portion of the not-self is taken and a portion of the Higher Self descends into our form. As we give this mantra each day, it affirms the initiation of the ascension within us, and eventually we, too, can rise into the ascension current, the Mother light, the Mother flame of purity.

I AM ascension light,
Victory flowing free,
All of good won at last
For all eternity.

I AM light, all weights are gone.
Into the air I raise;
To all I pour with full God-power
My wondrous song of praise.

All hail! I AM the living Christ,
The ever-loving One.
Ascended now with full God-power,
I AM a blazing Sun!

KEYS TO THE KINGDOM

CHAPTER 5
MASTERS, ANGELS AND ELEMENTALS

*B*esides the order of masters and men, there are two other kingdoms of spiritual beings: the angelic kingdom and the kingdom of elemental beings. When God created man and commanded him to be fruitful and multiply and to take dominion over the earth, he gave him helpers to assist in the important task of expanding His kingdom. Angelic ministrants and elemental servants of earth, air, fire and water formed the cosmic retinue that accompanied man as he descended to earth, "trailing clouds of glory" and vowing, "Lo, I AM come to do thy will, O God!"

During three golden ages, man talked freely with his God and associated intimately with angels and elementals. Communion with all life was unrestrained, and cooperation between angels, elementals and men was unspoiled.

To man was given the assignment of overseeing the creation and working with God to plan, to design, to invent and to direct activities on earth. To the elementals, the builders of form, was given the important task of bringing into manifestation the intents of God and man. And to the angels was given the responsibility of ministering to the needs of both men and elementals.

The Three Kingdoms

The Elohim are the highest beings in the elemental kingdom. Under the Elohim are the directors of the elements, who in turn are in charge of the gnomes, sylphs, undines and salamanders—the elemental beings who take care of the four elements of the nature kingdom.

The archangels are the foremost beings in the angelic kingdom, which goes all the way down to the tiniest angel. This kingdom includes the cherubim, seraphim and other orders of angels under their leaders. Every ascended master has his own legion of angels who serve with him to amplify the flame that he tends.

The kingdom of the ascended masters is the order of the Christed ones, the evolution that we call the sons and daughters of God. Mankind are included in this order. Their destiny is to become the Christ. This order includes newly ascended beings as well as ancient masters who have manifested the Christ consciousness.

The three orders of the heavenly hierarchy manifest the threefold flame. The sons and daughters of God are intended to outpicture the intelligence of the Christ mind, focusing the genius of God for invention and creativity. They represent the yellow plume of hierarchy.

The pink plume of the threefold flame of hierarchy is the order of the angelic hosts. Their service is to amplify the feelings and virtues of God. They bring the qualities of hope, love, mercy, compassion, charity, constancy and all the virtues that we need to make it in life. The angels help us to amplify these feelings, and they often do this through heavenly music known as the music of the spheres.

The author of Hebrews tells us that God "maketh his angels spirits, and his ministers a flame of fire."[38] God created angels out of the very essence of himself. Angels serve on one of the seven color rays with their hierarchs, the seven archangels.

The elemental kingdom represents the blue plume of the threefold flame, the power of God bringing all things into physical manifestation.

The Seven Elohim

The seven mighty Elohim and their feminine counterparts are the builders of form. When God gave forth the fiat, "Let there be light," the Elohim were those who responded, and by their response, "There was light."[39] When God directed the formation of the cosmos in the physical plane, it was the Elohim who brought forth that creation.

Elohim is the name of God used in the first verse of the Bible: "In the beginning God [Elohim] created the heaven and the earth."[40] Elohim is one of the Hebrew names of God, used in the Old Testament about 2,500 times, meaning "Mighty One" or "Strong One." Elohim is a uni-plural noun, refering to the twin flames of the Godhead that comprise the "Divine Us."

The seven mighty Elohim are the "seven Spirits of God" named in Revelation and the "morning stars" that sang together in the Beginning, as the Lord revealed them to his servant Job.

Angels at Your Side

The angels would not only like to intercede for us but to work with us. And to work with them, we must get to know them, understand who they are and what they can do for us.

The word *angel* comes from the Latin *angelus,* which means "messenger." Every angel who comes to you is a messenger, whether of love, joy and peace or teaching, warning and protection.

Angels are messengers of light. They are extensions of the living Presence of God. God created angels to carry his messages to mankind, to be our guardians and helpers and to minister to our needs. They intensify feelings of faith, hope and charity, of honor, integrity, courage, truth and freedom, and every aspect of the mind of God.

Angels perform numberless tasks. There are guardian angels, angels of healing, wisdom, practicality, love and compassion. There are angels who attend our cycles of birth and death. There are even Christmas angels, to whom we

ELOHIM OF THE SEVEN RAYS

Ray	Elohim	Location of Their Etheric Retreat
1	Hercules and Amazonia	Half Dome, Sierra Nevada, Yosemite National Park, California, U.S.A.
2	Apollo and Lumina	Western lower Saxony, Germany
3	Heros and Amora	Lake Winnipeg, Canada
4	Purity and Astrea	Near Gulf of Archangel, southeast arm of the White Sea, Russia
5	Cyclopea and Virginia	Altai Range where China, Siberia and Mongolia meet, near Tabun Bogdo
6	Peace and Aloha	Hawaiian Islands
7	Arcturus and Victoria	Near Luanda, Angola, Africa

can call at any time of the year to bring the joy of Christmas into the world.

Angels see the big picture, and they work with us at all levels of our being. They know where we have come from and where we are going. They know that we have lived before and will live again. They understand the laws that govern God's universe, including the law of karma.

If you are blessed to receive a visitation from an angel, remember that angels have a mission. They have something to tell you. And you must listen. You have to ponder and meditate and be still for a moment and determine what brings this angel to your side at this particular time.

Angels have been present throughout the history of mankind, and they have a place in every world religion. The angels are still with us, but sometimes their presence and our ability to feel them and contact them is simply drowned out by the amount of "noise" that bombards us in our daily lives. Count the moments in your day when the phone isn't ringing, the television set isn't on and something else isn't going on all around you.

If you want the company of angels, make

KEYS TO THE KINGDOM

room for them in your life. For angels live in the world of Spirit, the heaven-world, and we live in the world of Matter. Angels naturally gravitate towards their home of light. So if you want the angels to feel comfortable with you, you need to make your world—your thoughts, feelings and surroundings—more like theirs. If you draw near to the angels, they will draw near to you.

This takes a little time and effort. It takes time apart to enter into daily meditation and to build a momentum on meditation if we want to have a more direct communion with the angels and with the mind of God within us. Angels can help us to facilitate that communion if we help them by taking some time to be alone and to still the senses. You may want to create a special place, even if it is only a corner of a room, where you go to meditate, pray and commune with God. What you most want to do is to feel comfortable with the angels—feel comfortable talking to them, praying to them. They do hear our prayers, and they do answer them as emissaries of God.

The angels have answered many an unspoken prayer or intense wish of the heart. You don't *have* to speak in order to get their attention. But you will get a more powerful response when you speak to them aloud. When you call to an angel in the name of God and in the name of the Christ, that angel is bound by cosmic law to help you. Using the name of God and his Son is a key to working with the angels.

The angels will do your bidding as long as your requests are in keeping with the will of God. If you ask something of an angel, in addition to your call they must also consider the free will of those for whom you prayed. Some will reject the prayer or the intercession, either consciously or subconsciously, and some will be healed or experience the intercession.

Almost everyone who has ever thought about angels asks the question: Why do the angels answer some prayers and not others? Why does one person pray for ten years without getting what he wants while another gets it immediately? Why are some houses destroyed by flood or fire, while others are left untouched? Don't the angels hear everyone's prayers?

Yes, angels do hear everyone's prayers. And one reason the response varies is because the angels' ability to respond to our prayers is based on the cumulative effects of our past actions—

our good and bad deeds from this and previous lifetimes. Yes, the word *karma* appears again.

The angels are neither genies nor Santa Claus. They also have to abide by the laws of the universe—including the law of karma. When we pray and give devotions to the angels, they can sometimes eliminate the effects of karma, but often they can only reduce them. And sometimes our souls need to experience some of the effects of karma in order to learn lessons and grow spiritually.

The angels hear all of your prayers. But in order for your requests to be granted, they must fulfill three conditions: (1) They may not interfere with God's plan for your soul (or with your karma); (2) They must not be harmful to you or to anyone else; and (3) The timing must be right.

It is important to pray for the right things and to ask for your prayers to be adjusted according to the will of God. And if you find that a prayer is not being answered, perhaps there is a reason. For example, you might pray for years to win the lottery and not win, because your soul needs to learn the lesson of earning a living and you have karma to balance with your workmates. But as you do your best in your job and pursue your spiritual path and work with the angels, you might get something you didn't expect, like a higher paying job that leads you in new directions. Angels always try to answer you in the way that is best for you and your spiritual path.

Archangel Michael—Your Protector

Jewish, Christian and Islamic scriptures all revere Archangel Michael, the archangel of the first ray. Jewish mystical tradition identifies him as the Captain of the Lord's Host who appeared to Joshua before the battle of Jericho, and also as the angel who guided the Israelites through the wilderness.

Archangel Michael and his angels of protection can answer your calls best when you pray to them daily. In answer to your call, Michael's legions can establish a wall of blue-flame protection around you, your family and loved ones. Even the words, *"Archangel Michael, help me! Help me! Help me!"* will instantly bring blue-lightning angels to your side. Send them wherever help is needed. No problem is too small or too great to be called to the attention of the archangels.

The following is a prayer to Archangel Michael that you can use when traveling in any form of transportation. You may want to make it a habit to call to Archangel Michael before you enter your car each day.

Traveling Protection

Lord Michael before,
Lord Michael behind,
Lord Michael to the right,
Lord Michael to the left,
Lord Michael above, Lord Michael below,
Lord Michael, Lord Michael wherever I go!

I AM his love protecting here!
I AM his love protecting here!
I AM his love protecting here!

The Other Archangels

Archangel Jophiel is the archangel of the second ray of illumination. He and his legions provide wisdom, illumination and understanding. They help you to connect with your Higher Self and assist you in absorbing information as well as dissolving ignorance, pride and narrow-mindedness.

Archangel Chamuel is the archangel of love. He helps us prepare to receive the Holy Spirit, developing feelings of love, compassion and creativity, dissolving selfishness, self-condemnation and low self-esteem. The angels of love assist in all kinds of relationships, whether on a personal level (such as repairing a damaged friendship or family problem) or at the level of world service (such as the healing of ethnic and racial tension).

Archangel Michael

Gabriel is the archangel of the fourth ray of purity and discipline. He is the Angel of the Annunciation, the one who announced the birth of Jesus to Mary, and who comes to announce the birth of the Christ Child within you. He provides guidance in creating your spiritual life and revealing your divine plan and purpose in life. He can be called on to dissolve discouragement and to promote joy, happiness and fulfillment. He and his legions can help establish discipline and order in your life. They promote organization in all types of environments, whether on a personal level or in governments and the world scene. Archangel Gabriel is particularly concerned with the halting of terrorism.

The archangel of the fifth ray of science, music and healing is Archangel Raphael. He and his legions assist us to develop wholeness, vision and spiritual insight. He brings the gift of truth. We can call to Raphael for help with the healing of the body, mind, soul and spirit and help in the practice of traditional and complementary medicine, music, mathematics, science and computer science. He repairs the rifts between nations, heals those injured on the battlefield of life and inspires new cures for diseases.

Uriel is the archangel of the sixth ray of service and peace. Among his concerns are the ending of war, bringing peace and promoting brotherhood and understanding. He is also known as the archangel of the judgment. He promotes inner peace and tranquility and the peaceful resolution of all problems. He renews hope and untangles knots of fear and anger in the psyche. He works with counselors, teachers, judges, public servants and all who serve others.

ARCHANGELS OF THE SEVEN RAYS

Ray	Archangels	Location of Their Etheric Retreat
1	Michael and Faith	Banff and Lake Louise, Canada
2	Jophiel and Christine	South of the Great Wall, near Lanchow, North Central China
3	Chamuel and Charity	St. Louis, Missouri, U.S.A.
4	Gabriel and Hope	Between Sacramento and Mount Shasta, California, U.S.A.
5	Raphael and Mother Mary	Fátima, Portugal
6	Uriel and Aurora	Tatra Moutains south of Cracow, Poland
7	Zadkiel and Amethyst	Cuba

Zadkiel is the archangel of the violet flame, bringing the qualities of soul-freedom, happiness and joy, forgiveness, justice and mercy. He can dissolve painful memories and negative traits and help us develop tolerance, tact and diplomacy. Like all the archangels, his world service is vast. Invoke him for successful negotiations and agreements of all kinds.

Pray to the seven archangels daily. There is no field of learning in which the archangels do not excel. With the Elohim, who are co-creators of life and form, they also have the power to create and to uncreate.

Archangels are extraordinary beings—nothing less than extensions of God himself, personified in form as God's grace and majesty and power incarnate.

Working with Elemental Life

Without the unflagging work of the elementals, we would not have a physical platform upon which to live. We would not have a place to work out our karma or to grow spiritually.

The elementals have the assignment of maintaining the balance of the forces of nature in the earth. Imbalance has appeared because mankind's karmic weight has been building up over centuries and millennia. Yet the elementals keep on working heroically to clean up the earth, the air and the water of our planet.

Day after day, they work to keep the earth on an even keel. Like mankind, they can become listless, tired, burdened and overworked. They can become bowed down with pollution and the weight of mankind's karma. If mankind will invoke the violet flame to clear elemental life of this burden, the elementals will be able to serve more effectively and bring a new harmony to earth and its environment.

Let us briefly look at the four types of elemental beings and their overseers, the hierarchs of the elements.

The sylphs are the air elementals who control the four winds, the atmosphere and the clouds. Under the direction of their hierarchs, Aries and Thor, the sylphs wash and purify the atmosphere and aerate the mind and heart and every cell of life. They are responsible for the purification of the air element, the atmosphere and the mental belt of the planet and her people.

Neptune and Luara are the hierarchs of the water element. They direct the activities of the undines, the water elementals who regulate, purify and balance the waters of the earth as well as the emotional bodies of man. The undines intensify the purity and flow of God's light in the waters. Since more than two-thirds of the surface of the earth is covered with water, the undines are kept very busy.

We have been asked to invoke the violet flame to transmute not only the physical pollution of the water, but also the collective unconscious of mankind and all darkness, disease and death that pollutes the emotional bodies of humanity and the waters of planet Earth.

The elemental beings of fire are called fiery salamanders. They serve under the direction of Oromasis and Diana to assist in the purification of the four lower bodies of mankind, freeing the physical body from the densities of impure foods, drugs and stimuli.

The salamanders are fiery beings whose auras ripple with the rainbow rays of the causal body. Composed of liquid fire that reflects the consciousness of those whom they serve, their appearance is constantly changing, for their chameleon-like natures instantly reflect the prism of the Christ consciousness that plays upon their forms.

Wherever there is uncontrolled fire, call to Oromasis and Diana and to the fiery salamanders to outpicture the will of God, at the same time calling for their freedom from the influence of negative forces that have imprisoned elemental life. Call to Archangel Michael to cut free the salamanders and all elemental life from the negativity and black magic that keep them from performing their service in full obedience to the will of God.

Virgo and Pelleur are the directors of the earth element, the mother and the father of the earth and the elementals of the earth element, who are known as the gnomes. There are billions upon billions upon billions of gnomes tending the cycles of earth in the four seasons, purging the planet of poisons and pollutants that are so dangerous to the physical bodies of man, animal and plant life.

The Body Elemental

One more elemental being is worthy of mention. Each of us has a faithful servant called the body elemental—a being of nature (ordinarily invisible and functioning unnoticed) who has served our soul from the moment of our first incarnation. His or her task is to tend the physical body. About three feet high and resembling the individual, the body elemental, working with the guardian angel under the direction of the Christ Self, is the unseen friend and helper of man.

Like all elementals, our body elemental does not have a threefold flame. However, when we have won our own resurrection and are ready for the ascension, our body elemental can be endowed with a threefold flame and ascend with us.

The body elemental has a consciousness, and its consciousness permeates your physical body. But you are the master of your body elemental. As you give him (or her) positive input instead of those complaining negatives, you will be much happier, more healthy and more holy—and so will your body elemental. And of course, your body elemental cannot do the best job, even though he or she would like to, when you don't provide the best food, exercise and spiritual practices.

CHAPTER 6
THE DARKNESS AND THE LIGHT

*W*e only need to read the newspapers each day to realize that all is not well on earth. While we see many people trying to bring positive change, peace and healing to the world, we also see others who bring hatred, fanaticism, violence and destruction. Part of our purpose for being is to bring the divine plan to earth, and when we seek to do this, we will eventually come face-to-face with the darkness that opposes it.

Heaven and Hell

We have spoken already about the heaven-world and the beings of light that dwell there. However, just as there are planes of existence with a higher vibration than the physical, so there are planes much lower in vibration. These levels are called the *astral* plane—a frequency of time and space beyond the physical, corresponding to the emotional body and the collective unconscious of humanity.

The astral plane has been so muddied and polluted by mankind's impure thoughts and feelings that the term *astral* is often used to denote negative planes of existence. And while the emotional body of the planet was intended to be the pure reflection of God's consciousness, we find that the pollution of these levels is far worse than is found on the physical plane.

Just as there are thirty-three levels to the heaven-world, so there are thirty-three levels of the astral plane, going down lower and lower in vibration. The lower layers of the astral plane are dense and dark places where evil and mischievous spirits may dwell. The deepest and darkest levels could be considered the equivalent of hell. These are the places where the darkest of the dark ones are found.

Forces of Darkness

Just as there are great beings of light in the heaven-world, so there are forces of darkness just beyond the veil who attempt to disrupt the divine plan of heaven. Their origin is described in the Book of Revelation: "And there was war in heaven: Michael and his angels fought against the dragon; and the dragon fought and his angels, and prevailed not; neither was their place found any more in heaven. And the great dragon was cast out, that old serpent, called the Devil, and Satan, which deceiveth the whole world: he was cast out into the earth, and his angels were cast out with him."[41] The tail of the dragon drew a third of the stars of heaven—a third of the angels—and cast them to the earth.

And so, millennia ago these angels who rebelled against God were cast out of heaven into the planes of earth—the four planes of Matter. They continue today as the unseen spirits (and some in the physical) who are the messengers of darkness, who oppose the light and the lightbearers.

Challenging Darkness with Light

Spiritual work must be done to challenge the darkness with light. Archangel Michael and his legions are the ones whose assignment it is to enter into this battle of light and darkness. As we call to them, we give them the authority to enter into the planes of Matter to bind and remove the fallen angels who inflict so much harm on the children of God.

In the late 19th century Pope Leo XIII released a prayer to Saint Michael the Archangel. It can be used to exorcise evil spirits that prey upon one's light and consciousness and for the clearing of many forces of darkness from the earth. As Michael cast Lucifer and the fallen angels out of heaven, so he is the key in the great spiritual battle that is still being played out in this world.

Here is Pope Leo's prayer adapted for the challenges of the present day:

> *Saint Michael the Archangel, defend us in Armageddon. Be our protection against the wickedness and snares of the devil. May God rebuke him, we humbly pray; and do thou, O Prince of the heavenly host, by the power of God, bind the forces of Death and Hell, the seed of Satan, the false hierarchy of Antichrist, and all evil spirits who wander through the world for the ruin of souls, and remand them to the Court of the Sacred Fire* * *for their Final Judgment.*
>
> *Cast out the dark ones and their darkness,*

---

* The Court of the Sacred Fire is described in Revelation, chapters 4 and 5.

the evildoers and their evil words and works, cause, effect, record and memory, into the lake of sacred fire "prepared for the devil and his angels."

In the name of the Father, the Son, the Holy Spirit and the Mother, Amen.

When you give a prayer or invocation such as this, you are surrounded by the communion of saints, the cloud of witnesses. When you go to your I AM Presence, the Holy Spirit descends as the Comforter. Archangel Michael and his legions respond immediately. Their Presence is with you. You can claim that momentum and power, backed by the ascended masters and the entire Spirit of the Great White Brotherhood. And you can make the call for the challenging of every darkness that comes your way or that comes to your attention. You simply have to make the call. Use the science of the spoken Word, and by cosmic law, ascended masters must come and stand in your aura. They can multiply their light body and place their presence over you and everyone and every place where the light is being invoked.

Judgment of the Forces of Darkness

Jesus is the great way-shower who shows us how to check the proliferation of evil on earth and to challenge the forces of darkness that threaten to overtake the light.

Two thousand years ago he said "For judgment I am come into this world."[42] And he told Peter, "I will give unto thee the keys of the kingdom of heaven: and whatsoever thou shalt bind on earth shall be bound in heaven: and whatsoever thou shalt loose on earth shall be loosed in heaven."[43] Today Jesus and Saint Germain give these keys to us for the binding of the fallen angels.

Ancient Tibetan manuscripts say that Jesus spent 18 years (age 12 to 30) in the East as both student and teacher. He mastered Hindu and Buddhist scriptures, learned to heal and cast out devils. In the East, Jesus prepared for his mission in Palestine and learned to invoke the light to deal with forces of darkness in the earth.[44]

He told his disciples before he left, "These and greater works shall ye do because I go unto my Father."[45] How can we possibly do greater works than Jesus? Only through the Christ within. We have the seed of Christ within us, and we can become more and more of that Christ light. And as our own Christ Self is reinforced by the Christ of Jesus, we can do those greater works.

There is an empowerment conferred by Jesus and the beings of light in heaven for the curtailing of evil on earth. The apostle Paul confirmed this empowerment when he told the Christians at Corinth: "Do ye not know that the saints shall judge the world? and if the world shall be judged by you, are ye unworthy to judge the smallest matters? Know ye not that we shall judge [the fallen] angels? how much more things that pertain to this life?"[46]

The True Meaning of the Judgment

When we speak of the judgment, we are not referring to being judgmental of others. In fact, the Bible warns us against judging another: "Judge not, that ye be not judged."[47]

When we pray for the judgment of forces of darkness, we need to be very clear who is doing the work. It is not our human self or our human personality. The Bible tells us, "Greater is he that is in you than he that is in the world."[48] He that is in us is the Christ light, the hidden man of the heart, our own Holy Christ Self. There is no instrument of black magic, no fallen one, who can stand before the Lord, the living Christ. But we need to be very clear that it is not the "little me," the lesser self, who is doing this. It is the Higher Self who does the work—Christ in me, God in me is the doer. We do not judge. The light is the judge.

Jesus warns that if we attempt to do this work and defeat the adversary alone, there is no guarantee of our survival. For it is by the armies of the Lord, by the coming of the Faithful and True,[49] by the coming of the Holy Spirit in the entire Spirit of the Great White Brotherhood that the children of light will escape these perpetrators of darkness.

If we do this work, we should also get to know Archangel Uriel, the Angel of the Lord's Judgment. His presence in heaven and on earth is foundational to the spiritual work of dealing with evil. Uriel and the other archangels stand ready to assist in the solution of all world problems including the ending of international terrorism, but they need our help and our calls.

The Seed of Light Within

When dealing with forces of darkness, we need to keep our eyes turned towards the light. It is important to focus on the seed of God in everyone, even our worst enemy. As we concentrate on that light and nourish it in ourselves and others, the light in the earth can expand to displace the darkness that is removed in the action of the judgment.

The problems of the world will not be solved by the United Nations; rather they will be solved by individuals united in God. One individual who is united with God can be the igniting and upliftment of a world. All the avatars and beings of light of all the major religions have taught that message in different ways.

You can aspire to that goal even while you work in any field or profession you feel called to follow—just as you can worship and pray in any form that speaks to your heart.

The Enemy Within

Each of us has a Higher Self and the seed of light within. We also have a not-self, which is known in esoteric tradition as the dweller-on-the-threshold. It is the anti-self, the synthetic self, the antithesis of the Real Self. It is also known as the enemy within.

The dweller is the conglomerate of the self-created ego, ill-conceived through the inordinate use of the gift of free will. It consists of the carnal mind and a constellation of misqualified energies, forcefields, focuses and animal magnetism * comprising the subconscious mind.

The momentums of untransmuted karma in orbit around the nucleus of the synthetic self form what looks like an "electronic belt" of misqualified energy around the lower portion of man's physical body. Surrounding the four lower bodies from the waist down, this electronic belt contains the cause, effect, record and memory of human karma in its negative aspect. Diagrammed at the point of the solar plexus and extending downward in a negative spiral to beneath the feet, this conglomerate of human creation forms a dense forcefield resembling the shape of a kettledrum.

Referred to as the realm of the subconscious

---

* Animal magnetism is density and negative substance in any of the four lower bodies.

or the unconscious, the electronic belt contains the records of unredeemed karma from all embodiments. At the eye of this vortex of untransmuted energy is the consciousness of the anti-self personified in the dweller-on-the-threshold, which must be slain before one can attain full Christhood.

The dweller may lie dormant within the subconscious and rarely appear on the surface of awareness as people lead lives in the realm of relative good, contacting neither the fullness of Christ nor the fullness of anti-Christ. But when the sleeping serpent of the dweller is awakened by the presence of Christ, the soul must make the free-will decision to slay, by the power of the I AM Presence, this self-willed personal force of anti-Christ and become the defender of the Real Self until the soul is fully reunited with that Real Self.

The not-self is subtle and cunning, and the awareness of it is one of the most important keys that we have on the spiritual path. In order to obtain the victory over the lesser self, we need to invite the assistance of the angels and the masters who have already overcome outer limitations and conditions. They are ready and willing to assist us.

Finally, my brethren, be strong in the Lord, and in the power of his might.

Put on the whole armour of God, that ye may be able to stand against the wiles of the devil.

For we wrestle not against flesh and blood, but against principalities, against powers, against the rulers of the darkness of this world, against spiritual wickedness in high places.

Wherefore take unto you the whole armour of God, that ye may be able to withstand in the evil day, and having done all, to stand.

Stand therefore, having your loins girt about with truth, and having on the breastplate of righteousness.

Paul to the Ephesians

CHAPTER 7
THE HEAVENLY HIERARCHY

The hierarchy of heaven is a vast network of masters, angels and cosmic beings working together with unascended mankind and elemental life for the victory of life on this planetary home. We have already spoken about the seven chohans, the seven archangels, the seven Elohim and the hierarchs of the elemental kingdom. Here are just a few other heavenly beings who work closely with earth and her inhabitants.

The World Teachers, Jesus and Kuthumi

Jesus and Kuthumi occupy the office of World Teacher. They are responsible for setting forth the teachings that will be the foundation for individual self-mastery and Christ consciousness in this two-thousand-year cycle. They

Jesus and Kuthumi

sponsor all souls seeking union with God, tutoring them in the fundamental laws governing the cause-effect sequences of their own karma and teaching them how to come to grips with the day-to-day challenges of their individual dharma (one's duty to fulfill the Christ potential through the sacred labor).

The World Teachers sponsor the education of souls in the Christ light at every level, from preschool through primary and secondary education to college and university levels. In every nation on earth, they have inspired teachers, philosophers, scientists, artists and people from all walks of life with the wisdom of the ages as it applies to each particular culture—even as the many cultures of the world serve to bring forth the many facets of the Christ consciousness.

They bring to mankind the teachings of the Cosmic Christ and the various stages on the path of initiation.

Sanat Kumara, the Ancient of Days

Sanat Kumara is a great master of light who came to earth aeons ago, at the lowest point of the planet's history. All light had gone out in earth's evolutions, and there was not a single individual who gave adoration to their God Presence. So great was their departure from cosmic law that the Cosmic Council decreed the dissolution of the planet.

Sanat Kumara came to earth in this darkest hour. He and the band of 144,000 souls of light who accompanied him volunteered to keep the flame of life on behalf of earth's people. This they vowed to do until the children of God would respond to the love of God and turn once again to serve their I AM Presence.

Sanat Kumara was the first messenger to the planet and the first Keeper of the Flame after the Fall of man and woman. His retreat, known as Shamballa, was established on the White Island in the Gobi Sea (now the Gobi Desert). The physical retreat of Shamballa was later withdrawn to the etheric plane.

The name Sanat Kumara comes from the Sanskrit, meaning "always a youth." He is known as the Eternal Youth and is also called by the prophet Daniel the Ancient of Days.[50]

The Lineage of the Ruby Ray

Sanat Kumara

Sanat Kumara and the masters who serve with him in the lineage of the ruby ray are the great teachers of this age. They come to initiate us on the path of the ruby ray of sacrifice, surrender, selflessness and service. These five masters are Sanat Kumara, Gautama Buddha, Lord Maitreya, Jesus Christ and Padma Sambhava.

Gautama Buddha attained the enlightenment of the Buddha in his final incarnation as Siddhartha Gautama (c. 563–483 B.C.). For forty-five years he preached his doctrine of the Four Noble Truths, the Eightfold Path and the

Middle Way, which led to the founding of Buddhism.

Gautama holds the office of Lord of the World (referred to as "God of the Earth" in the book of Revelation). At inner levels, he sustains the threefold flame of life, the divine spark, for all children of God on earth.

Lord Maitreya holds the office of Cosmic Christ and Planetary Buddha. He is known in the East as the long-awaited Coming Buddha who will come to inaugurate a New Age of peace and brotherhood.

Maitreya says, "I am the Buddha of the Aquarian cycle."[51] This *is* the age of his coming, and he has come to the fore to teach all who have departed from the way of the Great Guru, Sanat Kumara, from whose lineage both he and Gautama descended.

Maitreya attained the Christ consciousness many centuries prior to the final incarnation of Jesus. He sponsored Jesus and was his teacher, and was the one (in addition to Jesus' own I AM Presence) whom Jesus called Father.

He focuses the radiance of the Cosmic Christ to the evolutions of earth. He is guardian to the planet Earth from Venus, and his name means "loving kindness." He is also known as the great initiator, for he initiates us in cosmic cycles and supervises our initiation on the spiritual path.

Jesus Christ came 2,000 years ago to demonstrate a path of Christhood that all could walk in this age. We know him today as the ascended master and World Teacher, and he is once more looking for disciples who would walk the path with him and know the victory of the ascension.

Padma Sambhava is revered throughout the Himalayan countries as the "Precious Guru." He is the founder of Tibetan Buddhism, and his followers venerate him as the "second Buddha." Padma Sambhava's name means literally "Lotus-Born One." He is a great devotee of Jesus Christ and Gautama Buddha. El Morya has said that seeking oneness with Jesus is important for all spiritual seekers, and we can pursue that oneness through Padma Sambhava.

The Karmic Board

The law of karma is a universal law, and all in time receive the fruit of their sowing, both good and ill. However, cycles of karma may be lengthened and shortened, and karma may even be set aside for a time through the law of forgiveness. At various times, Jesus and many other members of the Brotherhood have stepped forward to stand between mankind and their returning karma. They have offered to bear the burden so that mankind would not fall beneath the weight of their karma.

The law is impersonal in principle, but it is personal in its application, and there are great beings of light who adjudicate karma and forgiveness, mercy and judgment for the earth and for each lifestream. Those who are responsible for these matters in this system of worlds are known as the Karmic Board.

All souls pass before the Karmic Board before each incarnation on earth to receive their assignment and karmic allotment for that lifetime. They also pass before the Karmic Board at the conclusion of each life to review their performance. Many people who have gone through a near-death experience have reported going through such a life-review before their decision to return.

The members of the Karmic Board are the Great Divine Director; the Goddess of Liberty; Ascended Lady Master Nada; Elohim Cyclopea;

Pallas Athena, the Goddess of Truth; Portia, the Goddess of Justice; Kuan Yin, the Goddess of Mercy; and Vairochana, one of the Five Dhyani Buddhas.

The Lords of Karma adjudicate the cycles of individual karma, group karma, national karma and world karma, always seeking to apply the Law in the way that will give people the best opportunity to make spiritual progress. When the Karmic Lords release a spiral of karma for the planet, the entire nature kingdom plays a part in its descent, which is always according to the law of cycles. The elementals have been the foremost instruments of the karmic return of mankind's discord. The earliest memory we have of this phenomenon is the sinking of the continent of Lemuria beneath the Pacific many thousands of years ago for the karma of the abuse of the sacred fire by priests and priestesses at the altars of God.

Twice a year, at winter and summer solstice, the Lords of Karma meet at the Royal Teton Retreat to review petitions from unascended mankind. Traditionally, students of the masters write personal petitions to the Karmic Board requesting grants of energy, dispensations and sponsorship for constructive projects and endeavors. The letters are consecrated and burned. The angels then carry the etheric matrix of these letters to the Royal Teton Retreat, where they are read by the Lords of Karma.

Students who are requesting assistance may offer to perform a particular service or work or make a commitment to certain prayers and decrees that the masters can use as "seed money" for something they desire to see accomplished in the world. They may also offer a portion of their causal body as energy for the masters to use, but such an offer must be approved by the Lords of Karma. The exact percentage will be determined by the I AM Presence and Holy Christ Self.

We have seen here a very small slice of the workings of the spiritual world. There are many other ascended and angelic hosts, Buddhas, bodhisattvas and cosmic beings to whom we can call and who work closely with us. You can find out more about many of them in *The Masters and Their Retreats*.

CHAPTER 8
TWIN FLAMES, SOUL MATES AND KARMIC PARTNERS

*A*s we develop on the spiritual path, our tests often come through our interactions with others. Through human relationships come some of our most difficult initiations and also some of the greatest joys in life.

We have many opportunities to work on these relationships. Throughout the centuries of our incarnations, we have had many roles: we have been father and mother, husband and wife, parent and child, brother and sister, associates in business, and all kinds of relationships in between.

Of all these relationships, the love between man and woman has provided the backdrop for some of the most intense and uplifting experiences. The ties of love are strong, and they exist from lifetime to lifetime. They have also been the cause of much karma and heartbreak, often forging karmic ties that bind beyond the years.

If we can master these relationships, they can be a source of great joy and much progress on the spiritual path. Understanding the different patterns of these relationships—twin flames, soul mates and karmic partners—can help us to make the most of them.

Twin Flames in Love

The quest for love and for the perfect partner in life is really the quest for wholeness. Each one of us, ascended or unascended, has a twin soul, or twin flame, who was created with us in the beginning. The twin flame is the other half of the divine whole.

Aeons ago, you and your twin flame stood before the Father-Mother God and volunteered to descend into the planes of Matter to bring God's love to earth. The original plan was to live through a series of incarnations on earth and then to return to the heart of God in the ritual of the ascension.

While on earth, however, we fell from the state of perfection by misusing God's light. Separated vibrationally from one another, we soon became physically separated from our twin flame by the karma of inharmony, fear and mistrust. Each subsequent incarnation apart from the twin flame was spent either creating negative karma, thus widening the gulf between us, or balancing some of the karma that stood in the way of reunion.

Now is the time, at the end of this cycle of history and moving into the Aquarian age, that people are again seeking to contact their twin flames. This search is prompted by our Higher Selves and is sometimes misunderstood at the physical level.

Twin Flames

Often when people learn that they share a unique mission with their twin flame, they begin to search physically for that one special soul instead of seeking their wholeness within. This is always a detour on the spiritual path, because it is our relationship to God and our Higher Self that holds the key to finding and becoming one with our twin flame.

Cosmic law requires that we first define our own identity in God before we can completely unlock the joint spiritual potential of our twin flames. For until twin flames achieve a certain level of mastery and oneness with their own Real Selves, they are often unable to cope with the weight of their negative karma as it is amplified in the presence of their twin flame. The same unique factor that gives twin flames their great spiritual power—their identical blueprint of identity—can likewise cause the amplification of their negative patterns.

While twin flames have a tie and a destiny at spiritual levels that is eternal, it is not always according to their divine plan to be together physically in this life. If the twin-flame relationship is not going to serve a spiritual purpose—if its reestablishment in this life is going to mean the breaking up of families and homes, if it is going to cause a cataclysm in people's lives because they are in different situations that they are bound to be involved with (because they are resolving past karma)—then often the outer mind would rather not deal with what the soul knows at the subconscious level. And so the outer mind does not readily admit to the "precognition" that is ever present with the soul.

Your twin flame may have already won soul liberation and reunited with God in the ritual of the ascension—or he may still be struggling to find the way. Where your twin flame is—what his or her state of consciousness is—can greatly influence your own ability to find wholeness. Because both of you share the same blueprint of identity—like the design of a snowflake, unique in all of cosmos—whatever energy you send forth is imprinted, or stamped, with that specific pattern. According to the law that like attracts like, all energy you release cycles to your twin flame—either hindering or helping him or her on the path to wholeness.

When you send forth love or hope, these qualities will uplift your twin flame. But if you are burdened with frustration or hatred, your twin flame will likewise feel the weight of these inharmonious feelings. Sometimes the inexplicable joys or depressions you feel are the moods of your other half registering on your own consciousness.

You can accelerate your spiritual progress if,

in your prayer, meditation and decrees, you call to your I AM Presence for the inner heart contact with your twin flame. You can make the following invocation:

In the name of the Christ, I call to the blessed I AM Presence of our twin flames for the sealing of our hearts as one for the victory of our mission to humanity. I invoke the light of the Holy Spirit for the consuming of all negative karma limiting the full expression of our divine identity and the fulfillment of our divine plan.

In saying this, even if you live in separate spheres, you can unite spiritually on higher planes and direct light into your own world and the world of your twin flame for the balancing of mutual karma. This inner contact magnifies the light and attainment you each have and releases the awesome power of the polarity of your love, enabling you to stand strong against the conflicts that inevitably come to the door of all who would defend love.

The use of the violet transmuting flame can also go a long way toward consuming the layer of karma that stands between you and your twin flame. That karma is just waiting to be consumed by the joyous, bubbling action of the violet flame.

Your mission, your twin flame and your ultimate reunion in the heart of God await you! And the reality is that twin flames are always united at inner levels, even if they are separated by outer circumstances. Your Holy Christ Self and the Holy Christ Self of your twin flame is the magnet that will draw you and your twin flame together—in this world, if possible, and in the next.

Soul Mates

The relationship of soul mates is a little different from that of twin flames. Soul mates come together because they have a mission together. They are working on mastering the same types of karma and developing the energies of the same chakra. Soul mates have an attraction that is based on the sacred labor and on the path of self-mastery. A soul mate is like the echo of oneself in Matter working at the same task to fulfill a blueprint for God. The soul-mate relationship is usually very compatible, although it does not contain the depth of the twin-flame relationship.

Mary and Joseph, the parents of Jesus, were soul mates sharing the responsibility for nurturing the Christ within their son. Both of their twin flames were ascended in higher realms of light holding the balance for their mission.

A soul-mate relationship does not have to result in a marriage relationship. However, a marriage of soul mates is often a harmonious match. Many people today who are still balancing karma but who are on the spiritual path find themselves drawn to their soul mates for the fulfillment of a shared dharma or sacred labor.

Karmic Partners

We may also have relationships with people with whom we have made karma in our past lives—good karma and bad karma. Sometimes the worse the karma, the more intense the impact when we first meet, because this is God—the God we ourselves have imprisoned through past negative activity—and we run to greet that one to set him (her) free from our own past transgressions of his (her) being. And we love much because there is much to be forgiven.

An intense negative experience of the past—such as violence, passionate hatred, murder, noncaring for one's children, one's family, something that you have been involved in with someone else that has caused an imbalance both in their soul and in yours and perhaps in the lives of many—is experienced as a weight upon the heart and an absence of resolution at the soul level. This is a very gnawing condition that troubles our consciousness until it is resolved by love.

In a karmic relationship, two individuals are drawn together for the balancing of mutual karma. When these relationships result in marriage, these marriages may be difficult, but they are important in achieving mastery on the spiritual path. The husband and wife may balance the karma they have together and thereby make great progress on the path. They may also gain good karma through a joint service to life or through sponsoring and nurturing their children.

Some of these marriages may give the opportunity to balance severe crimes of murder, betrayal or extreme hatred. Very often the only way we can overcome the record of hatred that intense is by the intense love expressed through the husband-wife relationship.

Not all karmic relationships end in marriage. Business partnerships, family relationships and other karmic connections also enable us to meet those with whom we have karma that requires resolution. The use of the violet flame may enable the balancing of karma without entering into a marriage. If, however, a marriage relationship is necessary, the violet flame can smooth the way and ease the bumpy places in the road of life.

Your soul knows why you have come into embodiment. You have been told by your spiritual teachers and your Christ Self: "There is this situation with so-and-so that requires resolution." At inner levels the soul who is on the homeward path (going home to the Father-Mother God) is very conscientious and desirous of righting the wrongs of the past—because she knows that righting the wrongs of lifetimes of ignorant and erroneous sowings is the only way to get back to the heavenly place we started from. And so, we long for wholeness; we seek the one we need to meet to find our way back home.

No matter what the situation, we can provide love and assistance, service and helpfulness to all those whom we meet. As we do this and use the violet flame liberally, we can balance our karma, whatever the source, and greatly promote our progress on the spiritual path.

The Marriage Union

God has blessed the human institution of marriage as an opportunity for two individuals to develop wholeness. Whether the union of twin flames, soul mates or karmic partners, the marriage of man and woman is a commemoration of the soul's reunion with the beloved I AM Presence through the Christ, the blessed Mediator.

The interchange of divine love in the marriage relationship is meant to be the same creative love of God the Father and God the Mother that framed the universe in the beginning. This creative flow can be expressed not only in physical union but also during cycles of dedicated celibacy as each partner goes within to commune with the I AM Presence.

The exchange of the sacred energies in sexual union is for the transfer of spheres of cosmic consciousness—an interchange of the light of causal bodies. The light energy resulting from this fusion enhances the positive qualities of each of the partners and strengthens their own divine identity, enabling them to carry their shared burden of karma. As the union is consecrated to the love of God, the harmonious blending of pure Father-Mother energies yields the Son, the Christ consciousness—whether it be in the form of a child, an inspiration, a successful enterprise or a work of art.

When this exchange is not spiritualized through a recognition that God is both the lover and the beloved, the two individuals may experience physical pleasure, but they may also unknowingly take on each other's karmic patterns without the benefit of a spiritually transmutative love. This may explain the frequent identity crises suffered by those who have intimate relationships on a casual basis—they take on so many karmic identities, effectively neutralizing their own, that they no longer know who they really are.

Relationships in Aquarius

There is no relationship—with friend, husband and wife, our children, brothers and sisters, relatives, professional relationships and co-workers—that, if it's going to endure, does not require work. We all have to give of ourselves in order to sustain a harmonious and loving interaction with anyone.

In our soul's acceleration toward Aquarius, we are winding up the loose ends of our karma with a number of people in this cycle of history. Karmic marriages and other conditions in life may come and go, and they are for a purpose. And we may experience more than one of these relationships.

The masters are not opposed to divorce if the inharmony is so great that more karma is made together than apart, or if the karma of the relationship has been balanced and the partners may now freely go their separate ways. However, so long as the karma remains (unless there be alternative means for working it out), these relationships should be binding.

While we are in the midst of them, we can make of these marriages a celebration on earth of our inner union with our twin flame. This is lawful. What is *not* lawful is to treat such a relationship halfheartedly or even resentfully and to not give it your best and the most fervent love of your heart. If you say, "Well, this person is not my twin flame, and this is just a karmic situation, so I'll give it a token effort and bide my time until the real thing comes along," that's a very good way to prolong the resolution of your karma and to make more karma.

What is important is that we look at life with the understanding that whoever we are dealing with *is God*. The person is God—in manifestation. The divine flame is God. The potential is God. And we must love that person with our whole heart, with the purest and highest love that we would have for God and for our twin flame. That love is liberating. It is a transmutative force.

We also need forgiveness in relationships. We need liberally to forgive others and to forgive ourselves, because that's the whole point of karma. We all have much to forgive and much to be forgiven for, or we would not find ourselves on this planet at this point in time and space.

So it doesn't matter if you're married to your twin flame or if you've ever met your twin flame. What matters is that you realize the sacredness of marriage and the relationship of man and woman, and that this polarity is always representative of the Father-Mother God.

Chapter 9
The Plan of Victory

The plan of victory for the children of God was nobly defined in the life of Jesus and that of many other avatars who have been sent by God. They are exemplars who point the way of freedom to generations who have lost their contact, not only with God but also with the heavenly hosts and the elementals. The ascension and the overcoming of every binding condition that must precede it are the birthright and the highlight of the life of all who are born of God.

When through service to life, an individual son or daughter of God attains mastery over outer circumstances, balances 51 percent of his karma and fulfills the divine mission that is the unique plan for his lifestream, he may then return to the throne of grace, being perfected in the ritual of the ascension. Once ascended, he is known as an ascended master. Here life truly begins, and man is ordained a priest of the sacred fire in the eternal, ever-enfolding service of his God.

All of life (hence, all of God) is in the process of ascending when it follows the divinely natural process of spiritual evolution. It is, therefore, through the ascension that angels, elementals and men find their way back to the heart of God.

We are urged by all of heaven to seek our own Christhood for many reasons. Jesus told his disciples that if they were to eat any deadly thing, it would not hurt them.[52] Such is the way of the saints. They can transmute anything that comes into their bodies and into the body of the planet.

Everything is possible with God. If enough spiritually adept people lived in a city or a home, that home or city could have a spiritual dome of protection placed over it that nothing could penetrate.

Perhaps that is how St. Paul's Chapel, only a block away from the World Trade Center, remained intact in the aftermath of the terrorist attacks on September 11, 2001. This amazing story was published in *The Boston Globe.*

St. Paul's Chapel is Manhattan's oldest public building. It contains the oldest known oil painting depicting the Great Seal of the United States, and the monuments and tombstones of some of the country's earliest heroes. George Washington visited this chapel in 1789 after his inauguration at the nearby Federal Hall.

When police escorted Rev. Lyndon Harris to St. Paul's early in the morning of September 12, he could not believe his eyes. Although buildings all around it had been destroyed and the chapel was surrounded by chunks of steel and rubble, somehow St. Paul's remained untouched—not even a window was broken. Rev. Harris said, "It's hard to say this isn't a miracle, the fruit of some divine intervention. I think it stands as a beacon of hope and a metaphor of good standing in the face of evil."

The chapel's pews quickly became beds for police officers, firefighters and soldiers taking breaks from their shifts. Hundreds of rescue workers were fed in the chapel, and it also served as a depot for supplies. Police officer David Capellini said, "It's amazing how peaceful this place can be, given how much is going on around it."

No doubt many took time to pause in prayer, and to read the words of a prayer by a soldier from long ago. Etched in bronze on the wall are the words of the Christed one, George Washington:

"Almighty God, we make earnest prayer that thou wilt keep the United States in thy holy protection."[53]

Plugging into God

If we are not plugged into God through the Holy Spirit every day and every hour of the day, we will have a hard time being able to stand up against the planetary forces of darkness, let alone solve the many problems that face the nations in these troubled times.

It does not matter if you are imperfect or not trained or not developed in self-mastery. God is the allness of you and in you. When you determine to turn your life over to him, to turn your body temple over to him, he can act through you and his angels can be with you. The times in which we live call for singleness of purpose. This is a time for all of us to plug into God and plug into our Higher Self.

When the Lord lets his mantle descend upon you, when your Higher Self, your I AM Presence, descends upon you, then you can have the empowerment of God to challenge forces of evil—beginning with those forces you have allowed to lodge within yourself and moving on to those that prey upon those nearest you. You can assist your loved ones and reinforce them with strength because you daily commune in prayer, in love and in service to your God. Wherever you live, in whatever city or state or nation, you are a pillar of fire.

You can keep the flame in your city! You can keep that candle burning! As the Master said, long ago: "Ye are the light of the world. A city that is set on an hill cannot be hid."[54]

KEYS TO THE KINGDOM

CHAPTER 10
ABOUT ELIZABETH CLARE PROPHET

*T*eacher, author, messenger, prophet— Elizabeth Clare Prophet's unique role stretches beyond the normal boundaries of the teacher-student relationship. With her late husband Mark, now the ascended master Lanello, she founded The Summit Lighthouse, a worldwide movement of the ascended masters, as a vehicle for the release of their teachings and for the betterment and upliftment of mankind.

In her role as messenger she has received thousands of messages from the ascended masters.

Messages from the Heavenly Realm

Mrs. Prophet describes the process whereby she receives messages from God, the masters and angels:

"I receive this prophecy through the power

of the Holy Spirit in the manner of the ancient prophets and apostles. When the transmission is about to take place, I enter a meditative state and attune with the Lord God or his representative. The Lord's Presence or that of an ascended master, a cosmic being or an archangel comes upon me, and the words and the light flow in a power and a personality not my own.

"This congruency of my soul with the living Word of God I call a dictation, for the words are being dictated to me even as I am speaking them in the vibration of the divine speaker. It is truly a divine happening of which I am but the instrument. It is a gift of the Holy Spirit and not something I can make happen…. The only way to describe this experience is to say, in the words of the prophet: 'The Spirit of the LORD God is upon me.' "

The dictations are recorded on video- and audiotape and released in the printed word as *Pearls of Wisdom*. A dictation contains the light and energy of the master. The spiral of light within the words is for your quickening and spiritual initiation. The teaching, when you apply it, can change your consciousness, being and world.

A Guru to the Masters' Students

In this age, through the mantle of the messengers, we have the opportunity to once again establish the guru-chela relationship with the ascended masters. This blessed relationship goes beyond the borders of this octave. It is a heart tie, forged by the love of the guru for the chela, returned by the love and trust of the student for the teacher.

The love of the guru and the chela is a love that is beyond the comprehension of the outer mind. In our original relationship with God we all knew the tenderness of this love, and yet, somewhere along the track of existence in the vast aeons of time and space, we left off the precious relationship of the guru and the chela.

The love of the guru-chela relationship is not understood in this world. In fact, it is often greatly opposed. The Hindu root of the word *chela* means slave. Those who attack the guru-chela relationship love to bring this up, because they point to the false gurus, who truly do enslave their chelas, with no love whatsoever.

However, it is truly enlightened self-interest to become the servant, the chela, of the true master. When we serve the master who is ascended, we are putting on his mantle day by day, his Christhood. We have said, "O master, I will help you to fulfill your karma, or I will help you to fulfill your dharma that is your mission and your duty on the planet." And the master is grateful because he needs hands and feet on earth. And so, if the master decides that you are someone with whom he can have a relationship of trust, the ties are established, and the light of the master flows to his servant.

The Mantle of Guru

Elizabeth Clare Prophet speaks about what it means to bear the mantle of guru:

"A guru is a spiritual teacher who not only teaches you about the spiritual path, but he or she also sets the example of how you must walk that path. Wearing the mantle of guru, I am the servant of the light of God within you, the champion of your soul. I am here to assist you and to uphold you on your spiritual path. I am here to help you find your way back to God.

"There is no greater love than the love that is shared between a guru and his chela. They give their life to each other in a sacred bond. Take the example of Elijah and Elisha recorded in the Old Testament. It is one of my favorite examples of the guru-chela relationship.

"God commanded the prophet Elijah to find Elisha and anoint him as his successor. Elisha was plowing with twelve yoke of oxen when Elijah passed by and cast his cloak upon him. Elisha renounced his former way of life and served the prophet.

"Years later, knowing that the Lord would be taking his master away, Elisha asked to receive a double portion of Elijah's Spirit. The prophet told Elisha that if he saw Elijah as he was being taken from him, then Elisha would indeed receive that double portion.

"As the two walked together talking, a chariot and horses of fire came between them, and Elijah ascended in a whirlwind into heaven. Elisha tore his clothes in two pieces and picked up the mantle, or cloak, of Elijah, which had fallen from his master. Empowered by the Holy Spirit, Elisha struck the waters of the Jordan with Elijah's mantle. The waters parted and Elisha crossed over.

"For thousands of years the great spiritual teachers of mankind have passed down their mantle and their teaching to deserving disciples. Around each successive teacher would gather students dedicated to studying that teaching and then becoming the living example of that teaching. Sometimes these teachings were written down. Sometimes they were just passed from teacher to student in an unbroken chain.

"With the transfer of the mantle from master to disciple comes the transfer of responsibility. The disciple pledges to carry on the mission of his master. In order for the work of the Great White Brotherhood to continue on earth, someone in embodiment must wear the mantle of guru.

"Today there are few true gurus in embodiment who are sponsored by the Great White Brotherhood. The lineage of gurus that has sponsored me, and whose teaching I am pledged to teach and uphold, is a special lineage in the Great White Brotherhood. The chain of hierarchy in this lineage follows from Sanat Kumara to Gautama Buddha, Lord Maitreya, Jesus Christ and then Padma Sambhava.

"Today the ascended masters present a path and a teaching whereby every individual on earth can develop his own one-on-one relationship with God. I do not claim to be a master but only the instrument of the ascended masters. Nor do I claim to be perfect in my human self.

"I am the servant of the light in all people. My books and teachings are intended to give people the opportunity to know the truth that can make them free. My goal is to take true seekers as far as they can go, and need to go, to meet their true teachers face to face."

KEYS TO THE KINGDOM

A Timed-Release
Capsule of Light

*W*e have had a twenty-five-year mission and more with these messengers. I could not give it to you all in one dictation, but I can place it in a capsule, a capsule of light as it were, with a timed release. But it is the release of eternal cycles, and it shall come through the flame in your heart, as my flame with your own, supporting transmutation around your threefold flame, allows you to awaken in the likeness of God.

Saint Germain[55]

KEYS TO THE KINGDOM

Mantras and Decrees

VIOLET FIRE AND
TUBE OF LIGHT DECREE
by the Ascended Master Saint German

O my constant, loving I AM Presence, thou light of God above me whose radiance forms a circle of fire before me to light my way:

I AM faithfully calling to thee to place a great pillar of light from my own mighty I AM God Presence all around me right now today! Keep it intact through every passing moment, manifesting as a shimmering shower of God's beautiful light through which nothing human can ever pass. Into this beautiful electric circle of divinely charged energy direct a swift upsurge of the violet fire of freedom's forgiving, transmuting flame!

Cause the ever expanding energy of this

flame projected downward into the forcefield of my human energies to completely change every negative condition into the positive polarity of my own Great God Self! Let the magic of its mercy so purify my world with light that all whom I contact shall always be blessed with the fragrance of violets from God's own heart in memory of the blessed dawning day when all discord—cause, effect, record and memory—is forever changed into the victory of light and the peace of the ascended Jesus Christ.

I AM now constantly accepting the full power and manifestation of this fiat of light and calling it into instantaneous action by my own God-given free will and the power to accelerate without limit this sacred release of assistance from God's own heart until all men are ascended and God-free in the light that never, never, never fails!

LORD MICHAEL, CUT ME FREE!

In the name of the beloved mighty victorious Presence of God, I AM in me, my very own beloved Holy Christ Self, Holy Christ Selves of all mankind, beloved Archangel Michael, beloved Lanello, the entire Spirit of the Great White Brotherhood and the World Mother, elemental life—fire, air, water and earth! I decree:

1. Lord Michael, Lord Michael,
    I call unto thee—
Wield thy sword of blue flame
    And now cut me free!

Refrain: Blaze God-power, protection
    Now into my world,
Thy banner of faith
    Above me unfurl!
Transcendent blue lightning
    Now flash through my soul,
I AM by God's mercy
    Made radiant and whole!

2. Lord Michael, Lord Michael,
    I love thee, I do—
With all thy great faith
    My being imbue!

3. Lord Michael, Lord Michael
    And legions of blue—
Come seal me, now keep me
    Faithful and true!

Coda: I AM with thy blue flame
        Now full-charged and blest,
    I AM now in Michael's
        Blue-flame armor dressed! (3x)

And in full faith I consciously accept this manifest, manifest, manifest! (3x) right here and now with full power, eternally sustained, all-powerfully active, ever expanding, and world enfolding until all are wholly ascended in the light and free! Beloved I AM! Beloved I AM! Beloved I AM!

MORE VIOLET FIRE
by Hilarion

Lovely God Presence, I AM in me,
Hear me now I do decree:
Bring to pass each blessing for which I call
Upon the Holy Christ Self of each and all.

Let violet fire of freedom roll
Round the world to make all whole;
Saturate the earth and its people, too,
With increasing Christ-radiance shining
   through.

I AM this action from God above,
Sustained by the hand of heaven's love,
Transmuting the causes of discord here,
Removing the cores so that none do fear.

I AM, I AM, I AM
The full power of freedom's love
Raising all earth to heaven above.
Violet fire now blazing bright,
In living beauty is God's own light

Which right now and forever
Sets the world, myself, and all life
Eternally free in ascended master perfection.
Almighty I AM! Almighty I AM!
Almighty I AM!

DECREE FOR FREEDOM'S HOLY LIGHT
by Saint German

Mighty Cosmic Light!
My own I AM Presence bright,
    Proclaim freedom everywhere—
In order and by God control
I AM making all things whole!

Mighty Cosmic Light!
Stop the lawless hordes of night,
    Proclaim freedom everywhere—
In justice and in service true
I AM coming, God, to you!

Mighty Cosmic Light!
I AM Law's prevailing might,
    Proclaim freedom everywhere—
In magnifying all goodwill
I AM freedom living still!

Mighty Cosmic Light!
Now make all things right,
    Proclaim freedom everywhere—
In love's victory all shall go,
I AM the wisdom all shall know!

I AM freedom's holy light
    Nevermore despairing!
I AM freedom's holy light
    Evermore I'm sharing!
Freedom, freedom, freedom!
    Expand, expand, expand!
    I AM, I AM, I AM
Forevermore I AM freedom!

I AM THE VIOLET FLAME

I AM the violet flame
    In action in me now
I AM the violet flame
    To light alone I bow
I AM the violet flame
    In mighty cosmic power
I AM the light of God
    Shining every hour
I AM the violet flame
    Blazing like a sun
I AM God's sacred power
    Freeing every one

THE LAW OF FORGIVENESS

Beloved mighty victorious Presence of God, I AM in me, beloved Holy Christ Self, beloved Heavenly Father, beloved great Karmic Board, beloved Kuan Yin, Goddess of Mercy, beloved Lanello, the entire Spirit of the Great White Brotherhood and the World Mother, elemental life—fire, air, water and earth!

In the name and by the power of the Presence of God which I AM and by the magnetic power of the sacred fire vested in me, I call upon the law of forgiveness and the violet transmuting flame for each transgression of thy Law, each departure from thy sacred covenants.

Restore in me the Christ mind, forgive my wrongs and unjust ways, make me obedient to thy code, let me walk humbly with thee all my days.

In the name of the Father, the Mother, the Son and the Holy Spirit, I decree for all whom I have ever wronged and for all who have ever wronged me:

Violet fire,* enfold us! (3x)

Violet fire, hold us! (3x)

Violet fire, set us free! (3x)

* "Mercy's flame" or "purple flame" may be used for "violet flame."

194

I AM, I AM, I AM surrounded by
    a pillar of violet flame,*
I AM, I AM, I AM abounding in
    pure love for God's great name,
I AM, I AM, I AM complete
    by thy pattern of perfection so fair,
I AM, I AM, I AM God's radiant flame
    of love gently falling through the air.

    Fall on us! (3x)
    Blaze through us! (3x)
    Saturate us! (3x)

And in full faith I consciously accept this manifest, manifest, manifest! (3x) right here and now with full power, eternally sustained, all-powerfully active, ever expanding, and world enfolding until all are wholly ascended in the light and free! Beloved I AM! Beloved I AM! Beloved I AM!

O SAINT GERMAN, SEND VIOLET FLAME

1. O Saint German, send violet flame,
   Sweep it through my very core;
   Bless'd Zadkiel, Oromasis,
   Expand and intensify more and more.

Refrain: Right now blaze through and saturate,
   Right now expand and penetrate;
   Right now set free, God's mind to be,
   Right now and for eternity.

2. I AM in the flame and there I stand,
   I AM in the center of God's hand;
   I AM filled and thrilled by violet hue,
   I AM wholly flooded through
      and through.

3. I AM God's flame within my soul,
   I AM God's flashing beacon goal;
   I AM, I AM the sacred fire,
   I feel the flow of joy inspire.

4. The consciousness of God in me
   Does raise me to the Christ I see.
   Descending now in violet flame,
   I see him come fore'er to reign.

5. O Jesus, send thy violet flame,
   Sanctify my very core;
   Blessed Mary, in God's name,
   Expand and intensify more and more.

6. O Mighty I AM, send violet flame,
   Purify my very core;
   Maha Chohan, thou Holy One,
   Expand, expand God's lovely sun.

Coda:* He takes me by the hand to say,
   I love thy soul each blessed day;
   O rise with me into the air
   Where blossoms freedom from
      all care;
   As violet flame keeps blazing through,
   I know that I'll ascend with you.

---

* To be given at the end of the decree.

INVOCATION OF ILLUMINATION

Living Christ within and round me
    Blazing 'lumination's flame,
Wise abundance now surround me,
    God-dominion ever reign.

Crown my brow with golden radiance
    From the wisdom of thy light;
Crown my doings with the evidence
    Of illumination's Christed might.

I AM, I AM the golden flame
    Of illumination blazing clear
From the heart of blessed Lanto
    In the Royal Teton here.

Blaze, O blaze thy shining radiance
    Through my inner being now;
Shed true light upon my pathway
    By a beam from wisdom's brow.

Light expand now to encircle
    Every nook upon our globe;
Come, bring every man your blessing,
    Brothers of the Golden Robe.

Living Christ now all about me,
    Blaze with all thy wisdom's power.
Thy truth blazing, none can doubt me;

Expand then in me every hour.

Crown my heart and mind with fire
    Kindled on thy altars bright;
Let a halo of thy wisdom
    Honor every child of light.

Hail, thou holy Royal Teton,
    Brothers of the wisdom ray!
Intensify thy golden radiance,
    Let the sun of light hold sway.

Come, Apollo, Lumina,
    Give wisdom to perceive
The perfect pattern for each life,
    Its way and means to weave.

Blest Jophiel, archangel dear,
    Set forth on wisdom's page
The edict that will usher in
    The coming golden age.

INTROIT TO THE HOLY CHRIST SELF

In the name of the beloved mighty victorious Presence of God, I AM in me, my very own beloved Holy Christ Self and through the magnetic power of the sacred fire vested within the threefold flame of love, wisdom and power burning within my heart, I decree:

1. Holy Christ Self above me,
   Thou balance of my soul,
   Let thy blessed radiance
   Descend and make me whole.

Refrain: Thy flame within me ever blazes,
   Thy peace about me ever raises,
   Thy love protects and holds me,
   Thy dazzling light enfolds me.
   I AM thy threefold radiance,
   I AM thy living Presence
   Expanding, expanding,
      expanding now.

2. Holy Christ Flame within me,
   Come, expand thy triune light;
   Flood my being with the essence
   Of the pink, blue, gold and white.

3. Holy lifeline to my Presence,
   Friend and brother ever dear,
   Let me keep thy holy vigil,
   Be thyself in action here.

And in full faith I consciously accept this manifest, manifest, manifest! (3x) right here and now with full power, eternally sustained, all-powerfully active, ever expanding, and world enfolding until all are wholly ascended in the light and free! Beloved I AM! Beloved I AM! Beloved I AM!

KEEP MY FLAME BLAZING

Keep my flame blazing,
By God's love raising,
Direct and keep me in my rightful place!

I AM Presence ever near me,
Keep me mindful of thy grace;
Flame of Christ, ever cheer me,
In me show thy smiling face!

PRAYER FOR PURITY

In the name of the beloved mighty victorious Presence of God, I AM in me, my very own beloved Holy Christ Self, beloved Serapis Bey, beloved Archangel Gabriel, beloved Cyclopea, Great Silent Watcher, beloved Elohim of Purity, beloved Mighty Astrea, beloved Lanello, the entire Spirit of the Great White Brotherhood and the World Mother, elemental life—fire, air, water and earth! I decree:

Beloved Serapis, in God's name I AM
Calling for purity's ray to expand,
Imploring that shadows no longer adhere,
So longing for purity now to appear.

My mind purify of its fleeting impression,
My feelings release of all impure direction;
Let memory retain the immaculate concept
And treasure the pearl of the
    holy Christ precept.

O souvenir of radiant wonder,
Let my mind on thee now ponder;
Christ discrimination, sunder
    All that's less than God success!

Cut me free from all deception,
Fix my mind on pure perception;
Hear, O thou, my invocation—
    My Christ Self to manifest!

O flame of cosmic purity,
From Luxor, blaze through me;
Completely clear all shadowed weights,
    Ascend me now to thee!

And in full faith I consciously accept this manifest, manifest, manifest! (3x) right here and now with full power, eternally sustained, all-powerfully active, ever expanding, and world enfolding until all are wholly ascended in the light and free! Beloved I AM! Beloved I AM! Beloved I AM!

I AM MY BROTHER'S KEEPER

I AM my brother's keeper.
O God, help me to be
All service and assistance,
Compassion just like thee!

I AM my brother's keeper.
O Jesus, by thy flame
Of resurrection's blessing
Give Comfort in thy name!

I AM my brother's keeper,
O Presence of God so near,
The fullness of thy blessing,
Pure Divinity appears!

I AM my brother's keeper,
The guardian of his flame;
In quiet power and knowing,
I love him in thy name!

CHRIST WHOLENESS

In the name of the beloved mighty victorious Presence of God, I AM in me, my very own beloved Holy Christ Self and beloved Jesus the Christ, I pour forth my love and gratitude to my beloved body elemental for his faithful service always. (Pause to visualize your precious body elemental in an ovoid of the pink flame of divine love.)

I now command my body elemental to arise and take complete dominion over every imperfect condition which may be manifesting within my physical body!

Beloved body elemental, move into action now to mend the flaws under the guidance and direction of my own beloved Holy Christ Self, beloved Jesus the Christ, and the immaculate design of my lifestream released from the heart of my own beloved mighty I AM Presence— O thou Great Regenerator!

In the name of the mighty Presence of God which I AM and by and through the magnetic power of the sacred fire vested in the threefold flame burning within my heart, I decree:

1. I AM God's perfection manifest
   In body, mind, and soul—
   I AM God's direction flowing
   To heal and keep me whole!

Refrain: O atoms, cells, electrons
   Within this form of mine,
   Let heaven's own perfection
   Make me now divine!

The spirals of Christ wholeness
   Enfold me by his might—
   I AM the Master Presence
   Commanding, "Be all light!"

2. I AM God's perfect image:
   My form is charged by love;
   Let shadows now diminish,
   Be blessed by Comfort's Dove!

3. O blessed Jesus, Master dear,
   Send thy ray of healing here;
   Fill me with thy life above,
   Raise me in thine arms of love!

4. I AM Christ's healing Presence,
   All shining like a mercy sun—
   I AM that pure perfection,
   My perfect healing won!

5. I charge and charge and charge myself
   With radiant I AM light—
   I feel the flow of purity
   That now makes all things right!

And in full faith I consciously accept this manifest, manifest, manifest! (3x) right here and now with full power, eternally sustained, all-powerfully active, ever expanding, and world enfolding until all are wholly ascended in the light and free! Beloved I AM! Beloved I AM! Beloved I AM!

COME WE NOW BEFORE THY FLAME

In the name of the beloved mighty victorious Presence of God, which I AM and by and through the magnetic power of the sacred fire vested in the threefold flame burning within my heart, beloved Lanello, the entire Spirit of the Great White Brotherhood and the World Mother, elemental life—fire, air, water, and earth! I decree:

> O Cyclopea, Jesus dear,
>   Mother Mary so sincere,
> Come we now before thy flame
>   To be healed in God's own name.
> Stand we in this place in time
>   Invoking now thy healing chime!
>
> Tone of golden radiance
>   Tinged with brilliant healing green,
> Pouring comfort through the earth,
>   Perfection so serene!
>
> Come, O Love in holy action,
>   Give us now God satisfaction.
> By the power of holy healing
>   In perfection's flame now sealing!

I AM holding_____ (name or names)_____
    Before thy Presence here;
Shed thy love ray forth upon___(him, her, them)___,
    Release thy blessing dear!

    And in full faith I consciously accept this manifest, manifest, manifest! (3x) right here and now with full power, eternally sustained, all-powerfully active, ever expanding, and world enfolding until all are wholly ascended in the light and free! Beloved I AM! Beloved I AM! Beloved I AM!

LIGHT'S TREASURES

1. Fortuna, Goddess of Supply,
   Of all God's wealth from realms on high,
   Release thy treasures from the Sun
   And now bestow on everyone

2. Whose heart beats one with
       God's own light
   The power to draw from heaven's height,
   Abundance to expand the plan
   The masters hold for every man.

3. Attune our consciousness with thee,
   Expand our vision now to see
   That opulence is meant for all
   Who look to God and make the call.

4. We now demand, we do command
   Abundant manna from God's hand,
   That now below as is Above
   All mankind shall express God's love.

BELOVED CYCLOPEA
BEHOLDER OF PERFECTION

1. Beloved Cyclopea,
   Thou beholder of perfection,
   Release to us thy divine direction,
   Clear our way from all debris,
   Hold the immaculate thought for me.

Refrain: I AM, I AM beholding All,
   Mine eye is single as I call;
   Raise me now and set me free,
   Thy holy image now to be.

2. Beloved Cyclopea,
   Thou enfolder all-seeing,
   Mold in light my very being,
   Purify my thought and feeling,
   Hold secure God's Law appealing.

3. Beloved Cyclopea,
   Radiant eye of ancient grace,
   By God's hand his image trace
   On the fabric of my soul,
   Erase all bane and keep me whole.

4. Beloved Cyclopea,
   Guard for aye the City Foursquare,
   Hear and implement my prayer,
   Trumpet my victory on the air,
   Hold the purity of truth so fair.

And in full faith I consciously accept this manifest, manifest, manifest! (3x) right here and now with full power, eternally sustained, all-powerfully active, ever expanding, and world enfolding until all are wholly ascended in the light and free! Beloved I AM! Beloved I AM! Beloved I AM!

DECREE TO BELOVED MIGHTY ASTREA

In the name of the beloved mighty victorious Presence of God, I AM in me, mighty I AM Presence and Holy Christ Selves of lightbearers of the world and all who are to ascend in this life, by and through the magnetic power of the sacred fire vested in the threefold flame burning within my heart, I call to beloved Mighty Astrea and Purity, Archangel Gabriel and Hope, beloved Serapis Bey and the seraphim and cherubim of God, beloved Lanello, the entire Spirit of the Great White Brotherhood and the World Mother, elemental life—fire, air, water and earth! to lock your cosmic circles and swords of blue flame in, through and around my four lower bodies, my electronic belt, my heart chakra and all of my chakras, my entire consciousness, being and world. (Include personal prayers here.)

Cut me loose and set me free (3x) from all that is less than God's perfection and my own divine plan fulfilled.

1. O beloved Astrea, may God Purity
   Manifest here for all to see,
   God's divine will shining through
   Circle and sword of brightest blue.

1st chorus: Come now answer this my call
   Lock thy circle round us all.
   Circle and sword of brightest blue,
   Blaze now, raise now,
   shine right through!

2. Cutting life free from patterns unwise,
   Burdens fall off while souls arise
   Into thine arms of infinite love,
   Merciful shining from heaven above.

3. Circle and sword of Astrea now shine,
   Blazing blue-white my being refine,
   Stripping away all doubt and fear,
   Faith and goodwill patterns appear.

2nd chorus: Come now answer this my call,
   Lock thy circle round us all.
   Circle and sword of brightest blue,
   Raise our youth now,
   blaze right through!

3rd chorus: Come now answer this my call,
                  Lock thy circle round us all.
                  Circle and sword of brightest blue,
                  Raise mankind now,
                  shine right through!

And in full faith I consciously accept this manifest, manifest, manifest! (3x) right here and now with full power, eternally sustained, all-powerfully active, ever expanding, and world enfolding until all are wholly ascended in the light and free! Beloved I AM! Beloved I AM! Beloved I AM!

Give the decree once, using the first chorus after each verse. Give it a second time, using the second chorus after each verse. Give it a third time, using the third chorus after each verse.

NOTES

1. Jeremiah 31:31, 33.
2. John 1:9.
3. Dannion Brinkley, July 2, 2000.
4. Exod. 3:14, 15.
5. John 1:9.
6. The Gospel of Philip 67:26–27, in James M. Robinson, ed., *The Nag Hammadi Library in English*, 3d ed., rev. (San Francisco: Harper & Row, 1988), p. 150.
7. The Gospel of Thomas, saying 108, in *The Nag Hammadi Library in English*, p. 137.
8. Arya Maitreya and Asanga, *The Changeless Nature (The Mahayana Uttara Tantra Shastra)*, trans. Katia Holmes and Ken Tsultim Gyamtso (Eskdalemuir, Scotland: Kama Drubgyud Darjay Ling, n.d.), p. 21.
9. Rev. 22:1.
10. Gen. 3:21.
11. Gal. 6: 5, 7–10.
12. Dannion Brinkley with Paul Perry, *Saved by the Light* (New York: Villard Books, 1994), pp. 18, 19.
13. Ibid., pp. 20–21.
14. Matt. 3:17.
15. John 7:38.

16. John 14:2.
17. Matt. 6:6.
18. John 1:9.
19. John 3:16.
20. John 1:14.
21. John 14:26.
22. Luke 24:49.
23. 1 Cor. 12:8–11.
24. Francis Johnston, *Fatima: The Great Sign* (Washington, N.J.: AMI Press, 1980), p. 139.
25. *Time*/CNN poll conducted in June 1996 by Yankelovich Partners.
26. Dr. William Nolan, quoted in Larry Dossey, M.D., *Healing Words: The Power of Prayer and the Practice of Medicine* (HarperSanFrancisco, 1993), p. 180.
27. James 5:16.
28. Saint Thérèse of Lisieux, *Soeur Thérèse of Liseux, The Little Flower of Jesus* (New York: J. P. Kennedy & Sons, 1914), p. 163.
29. Dr. Alfred A. Tomatis, quoted in Tim Wilson, "Chant: The Healing Power of Voice and Ear," in *Music: Physician for Times to Come*, ed. Don Campbell (Wheaton, Ill.: Theosophical Publishing House, Quest Books, 1991), p. 13.
30. *A Discourse on Abba Philimon*, in *The Philokalia*, comp. St. Nikodimos of the Holy Mountain and St. Makarios of Corinth, trans. G. E. H. Palmer, Philip Sherrard, and Kallistos Ware (London: Faber and Faber, 1981), 2:349.
31. Isa. 45:11.
32. Job 22:27, 28.
33. Exod. 3:14, 15.
34. Phil. 2:5.
35. Zech. 2:5.
36. Matt. 5:48.

KEYS TO THE KINGDOM

37. Luke 9:29.
38. Heb. 1:7.
39. Gen. 1:3.
40. Gen. 1:1.
41. Rev. 12:7–9.
42. John 9:39.
43. Matt. 16:19.
44. See Elizabeth Clare Prophet, *The Lost Years of Jesus* (Corwin Springs, Mont.: Summit University Press, 1987).
45. John 14:12.
46. 1 Cor. 6:2–3.
47. Matt. 7:1.
48. 1 John 4:4.
49. Rev. 19:11.
50. Dan. 7:9, 13, 22.
51. Lord Maitreya, November 21, 1976.
52. Mark 16:18.
53. David Abel, "Still Standing: A Chapel Spared Stirs Talk of Miracle," *The Boston Globe*, September 26, 2001, on-line version.
54. Matt. 5:14.
55. Saint Germain, "May You Pass Every Test!" in *Lords of the Seven Rays* (Corwin Springs, Mont.: Summit University Press, 1986), book two, p. 274.

RECOMMENDED RESOURCES

Books by Mark and Elizabeth Clare Prophet:

The Masters and Their Retreats
The Chela and the Path
Climb the Highest Mountain
The Science of the Spoken Word
The Human Aura
Walking with the Master
Community
*The Creative Power of Sound: Affirmations to
    Create, Heal and Transform*
How to Work with Angels
*Soul Mates and Twin Flames: The Spiritual
    Dimension of Love and Relationships*
*Creative Abundance: Keys to Spiritual and
    Material Prosperity*
Access the Power of Your Higher Self
Violet Flame to Heal Body, Mind and Soul

Books by Elizabeth Clare Prophet and Patricia R. Spadaro:

Alchemy of the Heart
The Art of Practical Spirituality
Your Seven Energy Centers: A Holistic Approach to Physical, Emotional and Spiritual Vitality

Books by Other Authors:

Wanting to be Born: The Cry of the Soul, compiled by Dr. Neroli Duffy, based on the teachings of Elizabeth Clare Prophet
The Path to Your Ascension, by Annice Booth

Audiotapes:

I'm Stumping for the Coming Revolution in Higher Consciousness
Spiritual Techniques to Heal Body, Mind and Soul
A Child's Rosary to Mother Mary

Opportunities for Spiritual Growth:

The Sacred Adventure Extension Course
An excellent step-by-step introduction to the teachings of the masters and their practical path of spirituality. The notebook contains instruction and spiritual exercises with an accompanying CD-ROM.

Pearls of Wisdom

Weekly written releases of the dictations of the ascended masters through their messengers Mark and Elizabeth Clare Prophet. Timeless releases of spiritual knowledge and understanding with practical keys for your daily life—directly from the masters' heart to yours. Past releases of *Pearls of Wisdom* are available on CD-ROM.

The Keepers of the Flame Fraternity

Spiritual seekers who desire to keep the flame of life on behalf of mankind can join this nondenominational fraternity and receive graduated monthly lessons of spiritual instruction. When you join the fraternity, Saint Germain sponsors your path of spiritual initiation and promises to assist you heart to heart in your homeward journey.

Summit University

Weekend or week-long seminars and spiritual retreats on a variety of spiritual subjects are offered in the United States and internationally. Summit University courses are also available on-line.

For more information about any of these resources or to receive a free catalog of books and products please contact:

Summit University Press
PO Box 5000
Gardiner, MT 59030-5000, U.S.A.
Tel: 1-800-245-5445 or 406-848-9500
Fax: 1-800-221-8307 or 406-848-9555
tslinfo@tsl.org

A NOTE FROM THE EDITORS

The material in this book is a distillation of the teachings of the ascended masters that Mark and Elizabeth Clare Prophet have delivered during their many years of service. Most of what is written here is compiled directly from numerous published and unpublished sources.

In some sections we have included additional explanation in order to give a complete and easily-understandable presentation of the teachings. If you would like to learn more about any of the subjects mentioned, we recommend starting with the books listed under "Recommended Resources."

We would like to close by expressing our gratitude to the two messengers for all that they have given us in their more than forty years of service. We hope this small volume will help make their teachings and the teachings of the ascended masters available to an ever-wider audience of spiritual seekers.

The Editors
Summit University Press

Mark L. Prophet and Elizabeth Clare Prophet are pioneers of modern spirituality and internationally renowned authors. For more than 40 years the Prophets have published the teachings of the immortal saints and sages of East and West known as the ascended masters. Together they have given the world a new understanding of the ancient wisdom as well as a path of practical mysticism.

Their books, available in fine bookstores worldwide, have been translated into 20 languages and are sold in more than 30 countries.